W9-BAU-450

MENNONITES IN THE CONFEDERACY

A Study in Civil War Pacifism

By Samuel Horst

HERALD PRESS, SCOTTDALE, PENNSYLVANIA

MENNONITES IN THE CONFEDERACY

FOREWORD

The Civil War was a harsh and tragic experience. For many Americans it involved bitterly conflicting loyalties in which hard decisions had to be made. For no group was this more true than for the religious denominations which adhered to a staunch Christian pacifism. In the South their situation was especially difficult. Opposed to war and rebellion as well as hostile to slavery, the Southern Quakers, "Dunkers," and Mennonites were constantly under suspicion as Union sympathizers.

Professor Horst relates the history of one of these sects—the Mennonites. Numbering only a few hundred families in the Shenandoah Valley in western Virginia, the Mennonites remained true to their peace principles. Although some were conscripted into the Virginia militia or Confederate army, most refused to bear arms or kill. In this stand they were encouraged by the determination of their Bishop Samuel Coffman, who ruled that those who responded to military service disqualified themselves for church membership.

Since Mennonite doctrine counseled obedience to the state except when its laws contradicted God's will, resistance to the government was passive and ever a last resort. Thus the Mennonite farmers performed various tasks for the South which did not involve actual fighting. And, unlike the Quakers, they were generally willing to employ substitutes to do their military service. In the middle of the war, after much church pleading

3

with the authorities in Richmond, religious pacifists were granted exemption, but conscription still remained a potential threat and source of worry. In addition, the social pressures, harassments, and even the occasional violence of their Confederate neighbors, drove many of the Mennonites to flee from the South. Younger men of military age, in particular, often had to go into hiding until they could cross the mountains and escape to the North.

Professor Horst tells the dramatic story of two of these refugee groups—"the seventy-four" and the eighteen —which were captured and then subsequently released. Amazingly "the seventy-four" offered no resistance when they were stopped by two Confederate pickets. This consistent adherence to the peace teachings of their churches later helped to persuade Confederate legislators of the sincerity of the Mennonite and Dunker conscientious objection to war. The final blow for these people came in the last year of the fighting when Sheridan's Union army carried out its systematic destruction of the Shenandoah Valley. Long burdened by the levies of the Confederacy upon their crops and livestock, the Mennonite population in Virginia, by this time much reduced in size, was ready to retreat finally within the safety of the Union army lines.

Professor Horst's scholarly study, based on a wide variety of printed and manuscript primary sources, taps new material and uncovers hitherto unused documents. His findings are an important contribution to a little-known aspect of Civil War history as well as a needed reminder of the quiet heroism of those few who were willing to stand steadfast for peace in the midst of the hate and carnage of war.

Arthur A. Ekirch, Jr.
Professor of History
State University of New York
Albany, New York

INTRODUCTION

This study is an attempt to relate the varied experiences of the relatively small number of Mennonites who lived in the South during the period of Confederate rule and to evaluate the expression of religious pacifism in connection with these experiences.

The flood of books and other writings on the Civil War especially during the period of the centennial celebration has produced comparatively little on the lives and experiences of those fundamentally opposed to the war on religious grounds. It is the hope of the writer that this study of one religious group taking such a stand will help provide some groundwork for future scholars in making a broader study of civil liberties in the Confederacy. The Confederacy was by its very existence a rebellion against the United States of America. How did a group which refused to accept the basic premise of the Confederacy, that is, the right to rebel, fare in a period when the Confederacy was fighting for its very life?

I began my research within the limits of the 1861-63 period. However, because more materials than I first anticipated became available, I was encouraged to broaden my study to include the entire period of the Confederacy and the Civil War.

A thorough study of Mennonites in the Civil War has never been made, either as they related to the United States or to the Confederacy. A study of this nature is necessarily somewhat limited because of the scarcity of official church records. Very few records were kept by Mennonites in Virginia a century ago and the records which are available are scant and brief.

In 1931 Edward Needles Wright produced his excellent study on *Conscientious Objectors in the Civil War*. Wright describes the religious groups opposing the war, the attitude of civil and military authorities toward them, and concludes with a comparison of religious objection to the Civil War with that made to World War I. He devotes most attention to the Quakers because of their numerical preponderance as a group opposing war, their active stand for unconditional exemption, and because of their more systematic and plentiful records.

Professor Harry Brunk has produced a very useful chapter on Virginia Mennonites during the Civil War in the first volume of *History of Mennonites in Virginia*. This brief treatment is the most extensive piece of work done on the subject.

A rich source of information exists in the records of the reports of the Southern Claims Commission concerning claims made by professed Unionists. Numerous Mennonites presented claims and the details of their answers to a standard list of questions provide important information otherwise unavailable. Professor Brunk utilized the general information tabulated by the Claims Commission but did not get into the study of the actual claims themselves. This writer did search all the claims of Mennonites he could find for information relating to his subject. Much more detailed studies should, however, be made of these.

This writer succeeded in locating other materials in the National Archives which apparently have never been used in writings on the subject.

Heretofore the scattered writings on this subject have tended to idolize the men involved in their experiences. Many stories have become virtually legendary. The Mennonite scholar needs to approach these with discrimination. In some, the details are confusing and occasionally inaccurate in their relation to historical fact. Most of these, however, are evidently basically reliable as to their general content.

Throughout this thesis I shall use the term "Dunkers" when referring to the Brethren, Dunkards, or Tunkers. Although all of these terms are used, in my research I found that the term "Dunker" was used most consistently to designate this group. Quite frequently, however, the term is used more generally and is meant to include not only Dunkers but Mennonites as well. This seems to have been the practice especially of persons from other areas who thought Mennonites and Dunkers to be the same group. The Mennonites and Dunkers, although similar in appearance and belief, were two distinct groups in terms of origin and organization.

This study has been organized along chronological lines. The first crisis experience for religious objectors came in connection with the creation of the Confederacy itself, the secession movement. In 1861, after the war was launched, many Mennonite men cooperated by going into militia service but refused to take life. This attempt at cooperation with the government proved unsatisfactory. In 1862 the men hid or fled to escape service. Two fleeing groups were arrested and their capture and imprisonment spurred church leaders to press the government for recognition of religious objection to military participation. Their successful attempts to secure recognition are revealing but their apprehension continued as the intensity of the war and the desperation of the South increased. The climax came in 1864 when a determined Union campaign under the leadership of General Sheridan systematically devastated the Valley, putting an end to its usefulness as a strategic area in the war.

I am indebted to many persons for their help and encouragement in this undertaking. First, I acknowledge Arthur A. Ekirch, Jr., my adviser and major professor in my studies at American University, who encouraged me to pursue the subject. A scholar in the history of civil liberties and a writer of experience, he has given me invaluable direction. Professor William R. Hutchison has given considerable help. I owe a debt to Harry A. Brunk, Professor Emeritus at Eastern Mennonite College, for the interest he has fostered in this subject in past years and for his reading over this work and his suggestions concerning it. Grant Stoltzfus, Associate Professor at Eastern Mennonite College, has provided constant encouragement in numerous ways. Other persons who were indispensable in my search for materials were Buford Roland, Archivist-in-Charge of the Legislative Records Section of the National Archives; William J. Van Schreeven, the Virginia State Library Archivist of Richmond; Robert Waitt, Jr., Secretary of the Civil War Centennial Committee for the city of Richmond; and Miss Agnes Kline of Bridgewater College. The members of the Research Committee and the larger body, the Research Council of Eastern Mennonite College, deserve to be mentioned for their help and encouragement toward publication. The patience and loyalty of my wife Elizabeth and my children were indispensable.

Much work needs to be done on the subject and further research and study will undoubtedly help fill out the details of the experiences of Mennonite religious objectors in the Confederacy and the significance of their role in this period of history. Such further study will undoubtedly help expose any errors of fact or interpretation which may be included in this study.

List of Illustrations

Section of Official Topographical Map 49
Castle Thunder 55
Rockingham County Courthouse as It Appeared
     During the Civil War 57
Bishop Samuel Coffman (1822-1894) 66
Dunkers and Mennonites Getting Passes to Go
     North 107
Official Topographical Map (foldout)
                              Inside Back Cover

CONTENTS

FOREWORD 3
INTRODUCTION 7
1. BACKGROUNDS 15
   Religious 15
   Political 17
   Military 19
2. THE SECESSION CRISIS 23
   Virginia Wavers 23
   Mennonites and Secession 26
3. RELUCTANT COOPERATION 28
   Early Military Pressure 28
   Early War Experiences 33
4. FUGITIVES AND DESERTERS 41
5. FLIGHT AND PRISON 47
   The Seventy-Four 50
   The Eighteen 56
6. STRUGGLES FOR RECOGNITION 62
   Virginia Provides Exemption 65
   Confederate Conscription Law 75
7. CONTINUED APPREHENSIONS 85
8. DESTRUCTION AND FAMINE 96
9. SUMMARY AND CONCLUSIONS 111
FOOTNOTES 116
BIBLIOGRAPHY 131
INDEX 139

Chapter *1*

BACKGROUNDS

I. RELIGIOUS

Mennonites have always emphasized the avoidance of military service in their attempt to observe literally the teachings of Christ to "love your enemies" and to "turn the other cheek." During the Revolutionary War Mennonites were generally respected by American officials for their peace stand although some were imprisoned temporarily. This struggle, however, never involved large numbers of troops. The War of 1812 with England and the later struggle with Mexico were not of sufficient duration to test their principles of pacifism. [1] The Civil War, however, was a military struggle on a large scale which called for hundreds of thousands of men on each side.

The Mennonites of the Confederacy were concentrated in Virginia, which until 1863 included the areas that now comprise West Virginia. For the most part they were concentrated in the section of the Shenandoah Valley which included Rockingham and Augusta counties. No definite population figures exist concerning the total Mennonite population. However, L. J. Heatwole estimated that there were about four hundred families in the Shenandoah Valley until the last year of the war when possibly as many as one hundred families left the Confederacy. [2]

The Dunkers, who also originated in Europe, lived in some of the same communities as the Mennonites. They seem to have outnumbered the Mennonites in the Valley. Relations between the two groups were somewhat strained in spite of their seeming similarities. The stress of the Dunkers on immersion as the only rightful mode of baptism could not be accepted by the Mennonites. There were other differences, too. However, as this study will show, there was considerable cooperation and Dunker leaders not only did their own people a great service, but aided Mennonites as well, by making persistent contacts with state and Confederate officials. There were Quakers in Virginia also, but the Mennonites apparently had little contact with them.

These three groups opposed not only participation in war but also slavery, secession, and rebellion. [3] Peter Burkholder, a Mennonite bishop, spoke out against slavery before the war and the Virginia Mennonite Conference prohibited the owning and hiring of slaves. [4] Although slavery was not nearly as dominant in the Valley as in many other areas in the South, Rockingham County had 2,387 slaves in 1860 and Augusta County had 4,700. [5]

Virginia Mennonites of the period adhered to the so-called Burkholder Confession of Faith which recognized the government as "an ordinance and institution of God" and held it to be the duty of

all faithful believers, to be subject to the higher powers, not only for fear of punishment, but also for conscience' sake. And should it be that such believers were, for the Word of God, persecuted by the government, so as to forfeit their property, or to suffer death, they are not allowed to calumniate, slander, or defame, or with weapons of war to oppose or resist; but by faith look to God, to whom vengeance belongeth. . . .[6]

In situations where the government

will pervert and misapply the power which is imposed on and given it by God . . . and will interfere with the offices of Christ and with His kingdom, which is of a spiritual nature . . . and will attempt to be lords over God's heritage, by compelling its subjects to do things contrary to the word and will of God: it is then that the faithful believers must obey God rather than man. . . .[7]

Evil rulers were to be obeyed except when their demands required disobedience to God. Even in such a situation Christians were not supposed to resist but willingly accept the consequences of their primary loyalty to God.

II. POLITICAL

American Mennonites for the most part lived in areas siding with the Union. Virginia Mennonites kept constant contacts with the larger Mennonite groups in the North and their anxieties concerning the drift toward secession in the South betrayed a definite pro-Union sentiment. This sentiment is made further evident by the attempts of many to escape to the North.

Mennonites in the South were never involved in States' Rights considerations and although they were agrarian in their outlook, as were most Southerners, they did not think in terms of sectional rivalry or Northern encroachment on Southern power. They could not approve of, or support what they considered to be a rebellion against an established government ordained of God. They do not appear to have had any grievance whatsoever against the Union at the outset of the war and if they had, their doctrinal position would have obligated them to refrain from opposition or resistance. [8]

Mennonites and other groups objecting to military service in the North were fortunate in having President Lincoln and Secretary of War Edwin Stanton as political leaders during the war. Lincoln expressed appreciation for the "good wishes and prayers of God's people" and spoke appreciatively of the principles of peace as expressed to him by the Quakers. Lincoln's Quaker ancestry tended to make him sympathetic to religious opposition to war. To those who petitioned for consideration he showed respect and patience and at times he used the prerogatives of his office to act on cases of special hardship. When Quakers in Iowa addressed him through Senator Harlan he wrote: "It seems to me that if there be one subject upon which all good men may unitedly agree it is in imploring the gracious favor of the God of Nations upon the struggle our people are making for the preservation of their precious birthright of civil and religious liberty." To another Quaker he wrote: "For those appealing to me on conscientious grounds, I have done and shall do, the best I could and can, in my own conscience, under my oath to the law." [9] In contrast, religious objectors in the Confederacy did not have a sympathetic president. Although President Jefferson Davis said very little as to his opinions, in the summer of 1862 when he received a delegation of Quakers, he expressed regret that there were within the Confederacy people not willing to fight and die in defense of their country. [10] Quakers found their most sympathetic response from top level government circles in the person of John A. Campbell, who served as Assistant Secretary of War. [11]

III. MILITARY

The Civil War is considered the first of the major modern wars in the sense that it was a total war effort. In terms of human lives uprooted, casualties suffered, economic costs and social consequences, it was a major tragedy.

In contrast with the North, the South early in the war faced the menace of invading armies and the occupation of their territory. The location of the Federal capital on the northern border of Virginia and the Confederate capital at Richmond, only one hundred miles to the south, dictated a major part of the military strategy of both sides—that of attempting to capture the capital of the enemy.

It was in connection with this strategy that the Shenandoah Valley, the section of Virginia where the Mennonites were concentrated, played a vital part in the war. As long as the Confederates held the Valley, or as long as they tied up sizable Union forces, they were effectively relieving the pressure on Richmond and at the same time posing a threat to Washington itself.

The Shenandoah Valley was also strategic as a source of food supplies. Its fertile limestone soil produced grain of all kinds, beef cattle, horses, apples, poultry, hogs, and garden crops. Its German and Scotch-Irish inhabitants were predominantly farmers; however, not plantation farmers. They were a more self-sufficient people who lived a frontier democracy in contrast to the eastern Virginia aristocracy. Yet they were Virginians, for the most part loyal to the Confederacy, and they furnished the bulk of Stonewall Jackson's own division. [12]

Both the Union and the Confederacy soon sensed this strategic position of the Shenandoah Valley so that from the very first month of the war campaigns developed at its northern entrance. "Winchester changed hands so often that it became kind of a shuttlecock between contending forces." [13]

Not until 1862, however, did the first major campaign occur in the Valley when General Robert E. Lee, who was placed in command of the Confederate forces protecting Richmond, assigned General T. J. (Stonewall) Jackson the task of carrying on operations in the Valley. With a force estimated at sixteen thousand men he subtly avoided a decisive battle with larger forces and by a series of surprise attacks put the Federals in constant fear for the safety of Washington. Some of the important battles in this campaign occurred in Rockingham County where most of the Mennonites of Virginia lived. Jackson not only succeeded in causing the Federals to fear for Washington's safety but hurriedly united with Lee's army in time for a series of powerful blows that drove the Northern army in retreat from Richmond. Not until late 1864 were Union forces finally able to neutralize the strategic value of the Valley as far as the Confederates were concerned when the determined General Philip H. Sheridan finally defeated forces led by Jubal Early and then carried out a thorough devastation of the Valley.

There was a high rate of desertion during the Civil War. Desertion from military duty always needed to be considered serious and although attempts were made to count it serious in the Civil War, in fact the practice was so common that the Union and Confederate governments could hardly afford to apply consistently harsh penalties. There were many factors which encouraged desertion. In the South men who were allowed to go home to harvest crops or chop wood for their families tended to want to stay home, where in many cases they were desperately needed. When captured and forced to return, they would desert again, some men deserting as many as three or four times. Deserter gangs roamed the country and raided settled communities from their mountain hideouts. Ella Lonn states that in "Virginia, had it not been for Mosby's Rangers, many defenseless residents would have been at the mercy of roving bands of deserters, turned bushwhackers, who had been left in the wake of both armies." [14]   Desertion increased as the war lengthened to the extent that Confederate generals were severely hampered in battle.

Chapter *2*

THE SECESSION CRISIS

I. VIRGINIA WAVERS

Public sentiment in the Valley in the months before the outbreak of war was in favor of moderation. In the 1860 election the state at large voted in favor of John Bell, the Constitutional Union candidate. John Breckinridge, the secessionist candidate, ran a close second. Rockingham County voted for Stephen A. Douglas, the anti-secessionist Democratic candidate, while Augusta County voted for Bell. [1]

South Carolina seceded from the Union on December 20, 1860. As late as April 4, 1861, after six states had followed South Carolina out of the Union, the Virginia Convention by a vote of ninety to forty-five voted down an ordinance of secession. [2]

During this period previous to Virginia's secession John Kline, the persistent Dunker leader, wrote to Governor John Letcher, expressing the Dunker point of view and including among his statements the words that the "general Government of the United States

of America constituted upon an inseparable Union of
the several States has proved to be of incalculable
worth to its citizens and to the world and therefore we
as a church and people are heart and soul opposed to
any move which looks toward its dismemberment." [3]
Governor Letcher promptly replied on February 1,
1861, by stating: "I . . . am gratified to find that our
views upon public questions are so nearly in accordance.
I have never doubted that I would . . . be sustained
by the reflecting and conservative men in all sections
of our State. . . ."[4]

The attitude of Virginians toward the Union changed
drastically after the attack by the Confederates on Fort
Sumter on April 12, 1861, and the resulting call for
troops by President Lincoln from the still loyal upper
South. Virginia's governor, John Letcher, answered Lincoln's call with a blunt refusal and on the next day
(April 17) the Virginia Convention passed an ordinance
of secession. [5]   Virginia abruptly left the Union she
had done so much to help create. There only remained
the popular referendum on the convention's decision
which was announced for May 23, 1861. Prominent
"Union" men in Virginia such as John Baldwin of
Augusta County promptly sided with Governor Letcher
assuming that war was the only alternative. [6]   An editorial in the *Register* on May 17, 1861, appealed for
a vote for secession:

> We have heard that some of our peaceful, orderly,
> law-loving fellow citizens, the Germans will vote
> against it, or not vote at all. We cannot believe

this. They love their country, and desire its peace and welfare too much to do this. . . . Let not a vote be cast to give Lincoln this encouragement. [7]

Another editorial in the same issue stated:

We are credibly informed that a few contemptible Union shriekers who snuff in the breeze the coming wrath of an outraged and indignant people are secretly at work, endeavoring to delude men to voting against the ordinance of secession. . . . They are traitors of the deepest dye. . . . They should be hung as high as Haman. [8]

On April 21, Dunker Elder John Kline briefly described the tense situation as follows:

Great excitement on account of secession and war movements. The volunteers are being called out to enter the field of war and God only knows what the end will be. There is great commotion everywhere in the realm of thought and sentiment, men's hearts failing them for fear, the sea and the waves of human passion roaring. [9]

For all practical purposes, however, Virginia was already out of the Union, for on April 25 she ratified the Confederate Constitution and on May 8 was admitted into the Confederacy. However, it was this referendum which brought to a head the long-standing cleavage between Virginia's eastern and western counties, the latter voting against secession both in the convention and in the referendum and beginning a new state movement which led to the departure of the western counties into the Union as West Virginia. [10]

II. MENNONITES AND SECESSION

Early in 1861 there appeared an article in the local newspaper in defense of the Mennonites and Dunkers of Rockingham County. The local editor expressed resentment at the reaction to their early moderate stand on the part of the editor of the *Richmond Whig,* and he defended the Mennonites and Dunkers as follows:

> We know these people, we have mingled with them day after day for years, and we know that a people more loyal to the Constitution and the laws cannot be found anywhere. . . . They carefully and promptly pay their taxes to support the government which protects the slave holders as well as themselves. [11]

The high esteem with which these people were held, as this editorial indicates, must have made it all the more difficult to take an unpopular attitude in the months and years to follow. Many of the persons who after the war presented claims for property losses to the Civil War Claims Commission [12]   tell about the pressures which were applied to them at the time of the popular referendum on secession. The frequency of references to the threats made and their consistency show that undoubtedly these pressures were very real.

Some Mennonites did not vote for or against secession. Among these were Samuel Shank, Samuel Coffman, Daniel J. Good, Peter Blosser, David C. Breneman, [13] and John Geil. [14]   More outstanding are the cases of those who voted against secession, namely, Jacob Wenger, who claimed that he was one of eleven who voted against secession in spite of threats of hanging. [15] Henry Beery and Joseph Beery voted against secession.[16] It appears that those who were persuaded to ratify the decision of the Convention were more numerous. Among these were the following persons and the stated reasons for their action: [17]

John Brunk—to protect himself and his property.
David Driver—persuasion from neighbors.
Daniel P. Good—threatened to be hung if he did not vote.
Abraham D. Heatwole—persuasion and intimidation.
Gabriel D. Heatwole—intimidated by threats to be hung or shot.
Simeon Heatwole—voted under pressure.
David E. Rhodes—fear of reprisal for not voting.
Frederick S. Rhodes—intimidated by threats of violence.
Henry L. Rhodes—to protect himself and family from violence.
Jacob Shank, Jr.—persuaded to vote for secession.
Emanuel Suter—no reason given.
Noah Wenger—fear of injury and confiscation of property.

Although pressures were apparently applied to those reluctant to support secession throughout the area, this pressure appears to have been most pronounced at Mount Crawford where armed men were reported to have been stationed who not only threatened but actually did force individuals back to the polls compelling them to change their votes. [18]

Chapter *3*

RELUCTANT COOPERATION

I. EARLY MILITARY PRESSURE

The prewar militia system of Virginia required all males from eighteen to forty-five years of age to drill several times a year unless exempted. There was no exemption for persons who professed conscientious scruples against military activites. Most Mennonites and Dunkers would not attend these drills but would instead pay a nominal fine of fifty or seventy-five cents. [1]

When the war broke out in the spring of 1861, the militia was called and Mennonites whose names were on the muster rolls found themselves no longer excused by paying muster fines. Captain P. R. Bright of Company No. 1 of the 58th Virginia Militia Regiment wrote to Governor Letcher on June 6, 1861, as follows: "I have quite a number of men under my command who are opposed from religious scruples to performing military duty and invariably pay their respective fines, rather than attend to company drills." [2]

No reply from the governor to Captain Bright has been found. On a Sunday morning sometime in June, 1861, however, an unnamed captain came to Weavers Church and announced that all men between eighteen and forty-five should report the following week. An account describing this event states that the whole congregation was in tears. 3   Mennonite young men were placed in a serious dilemma, for to refuse to go into the military service meant deliberately assuming the position of deserters which for all they knew would result in a court-martial and possible execution for treason. On the other hand, to enter military service would appear to be unfaithful to the church.

Most of the men went into the militia under protest, vowing among themselves, to their families, and to the church that they would not use weapons placed in their hands to kill the enemy. 4   Some of the men chose to hide in the mountains, visiting their families at night. How many men went into Confederate service without any protest is not known. Margaret H. Rhodes lost two nephews who were in the Confederate service for some time. 5   Melchiah Breneman became a cavalry man and served in this capacity for over three years during which time he had three horses shot out from under him, each time escaping with his life. On the day before the Battle of Gettysburg he was shot in his left side although not fatally. About eight months before the close of the war he deserted. 6

The *Compiled Service Records of Confederate Soldiers*, preserved in the National Archives, are for the most part very scant in detailed information on individual service records. [7] This writer was, however, able to identify more or less clearly the following individuals as Mennonites or from Mennonite homes.

Name	Regiment	Enlistment	Remarks
Brunk, Samuel [8]	146 Va. Militia Co. A	July 8, 1861	Discharged Nov. 29, 186-, to work on Baltimore R.R. until otherwise ordered
Geil John [9]	146 Va. Militia Co. F	July 14, 1861	No further information
Good, Christian [10]	146 Va. Militia Co. G	July 8, 1861	No further information
Heatwole, Gabriel [11]	58 Va. Militia Co. D	July 25, 1861	Reported on Dec. 31, 1861, as dismissed and as having left the brigade district
Heatwole, John D. [12]	33 Va. Infantry Co. I	June 22, 1861	Aug. 31, 1861, reported sick in camp; Oct. 31, 1862, reported absent without leave since Aug. 12, 1862; Dec. 31, 1862, reported as deserted on Aug. 12, 1862
Heatwole, Shem S.	58 Va. Militia Co. G	July 22, 1861	Never reported as present on muster rolls
Rhodes, Frederick	146 Va. Militia Co. A	July 15, 1861	On Dec. 31, 1861, reported discharged for five months
Rhodes, Henry A.	146 Va. Militia Co. D	July 4, 186-	Discharged Aug. 13, 186-; obtained mail contract
Shank, Michael [13]	97 Va. Militia Co. D.	July 12, 1861	No further information
Wenger, Jacob [14]	58 Va. Militia Co. E	Dec. 9, 1861	No further information

Other individuals, whose membership with the Mennonite Church is uncertain but who likely came from Mennonite homes, were:

Name	Regiment	Enlistment	Remarks
Frank, David [15]	58 Va. Militia Co. G	July 22, 1861	Discharged July 28, 1861; exempted because of illness
Heatwole, Peter S. [16]	58 Va. Militia Co. G	July 22, 1861	Never reported as present on muster rolls
Heatwole, Manassas [17]	52 Va. Infantry Co. F	April 28, 1862	Absent without leave from May 8, 1862, to Sept. 26, 1862; present at Feb. 28, 1863, muster roll; absent without leave since July 28, 1863; appears on a Consolidated Descriptive Roll of Rebel Deserters within the Dept. of W. Va.; reported to Lt. Tennent; sent north via New Creek, W. Va.; appears on a receipt roll for clothing issued on Jan. 29, 1863
Suter, Jacob [18]	52 Va. Infantry Co. F	April 21, 1862	Absent without leave May 20 to Sept. 20, 1862; absent without leave on June 21, 1864; deserted Sept. 1, 1864; reported as a deserter from rebel army who came to New Creek, W. Va., and took oath of allegiance to the U.S. Government during Oct. 1864; farmer, age 21, from Rockingham County
Wenger, Henry	58 Va. Militia Co. H	July 24, 1861	Discharged Aug. 24, 1861; exempted on Surgeon's certificate
Wenger, Henry M. [19]	52 Va. Infantry Co. F	April 20, 1862	Deserted June 6, 1862; age 32
Weaver, David [20]	58 Va. Militia Co. E	July 22, 1861	Not present for muster rolls; making wages for the government

The militia companies formed from Valley recruits assembled at designated points [21]   and traveled by wagon to Mount Jackson. From this point they apparently traveled by the Manassas Gap Railroad which had been completed south to Mount Jackson before the war. [22]   In the vicinity of Winchester the men were placed in camps comprised of regiments involved in early operations concerned with protecting the strategic Valley area from Union invasion. Naturally they were expected to fight the enemy like others in their regiments. But descriptions by persons involved or by persons who knew them have been left which indicate an unwillingness to fight. Heatwole states that some of the men "were threatened to the point of being court-martialed and shot." When these tactics proved unavailing, some of them were eventually detailed to care for the sick and wounded and to serve as cooks and teamsters. [23]   Others were placed in the guard-house. [24]

That these men were not overwhelmed by their plight is evidenced by their resort to singing in camp. L. J. Heatwole refers to their off duty practice of meeting to sing familiar church hymns. Specifically mentioned are the hymns "O For a Closer Walk with God" and "Am I a Soldier of the Cross." [25]

P. S. Hartman has related the following concerning Christian Good.

> . . . Christ Good told me over and over he was forced into battle but he would not shoot anybody. At the first battle the captain came up and asked

him if he shot. He said, "No, I did not shoot."
Sometime afterward he got into another battle. After
it was over the captain came to him and asked him
whether he shot. He said, "No, I didn't see anything to shoot at." The captain asked, "Why, didn't
you see all those Yankees over there?" "No, they're
people; we don't shoot people." [26]

Edith Wenger Morgan relates the following experience (according to one source, not confirmed elsewhere):

My grandfather [Jacob Wenger] was drafted into
the Confederate army. Father [S. B. Wenger] remembers when the recruiting officer, Sem Bowers,
came and told him, "You'll have to go, Mr. Wenger,
you'll have to go." He remembers how his mother
cried. When the appointed day came, my grandfather reported at that appointed place, but told the
officers, "I promise you I will not hurt anybody. I
believe that war is wrong. I will carry the gun,
since you compel me to, but I will be sure to aim
so it will not harm anybody."

To punish him they made him carry big piles of
rocks from one place to another and then back again;
but when they found they could not break his will
they dismissed him. [27]

Wenger was arrested for failure to perform his
military duty and put in the guardhouse. [28]   P. S.
Hartman told of Michael Shank refusing to go into
service, and of the soldiers taking him out of his
house and hauling him on a wagon to Winchester. [29]

II. EARLY WAR EXPERIENCES

Word of the refusal of these men, as well as of

others of the Dunker and Quaker faith, to cooperate in military activities eventually reached General Jackson. On March 21, 1862, he wrote to Colonel S. Bassett French, Aide-de-Camp to Governor John Letcher of Virginia, as follows:

There are three religious denominations in this military district who are opposed to war. Eighteen were recently arrested in endeavoring to make their escape through Pendleton County to the enemy. Those who do not desert will, to some extent, hire substitutes, others will turn out in obedience to Governor's call, but I understand some of them will say they will not "shoot." They can be made to fire but can very easily take bad aim. So for the purpose of giving to this command the highest degree of efficiency, and securing loyal feelings and cooperation, I have, as these noncombatants are said to be good teamsters and faithful to their promises, determined to organize them into companies of one hundred men each, rank and file, and after mustering them, with the legal number of company officers, into service, assign them to the various staff departments without issuing arms to them; but if at any time they have insufficient labor to have them drilled so that, in case circumstances should justify it, arms may be given them. If these men are, as represented to me, faithful laborers and careful of property, this arrangement will not only enable many volunteers to return to the ranks, but will also save many valuable horses and other public property in addition to arms. It may be that officers for these companies would be useless expense. Please inform me as to the Governor's decision as to whether it is obligatory on me to assign them officers. All I have pledged myself is that as far as practicable I will employ them in other ways than fighting, but with the condition that they shall act in good faith with me and not permit persons to use their names for the purpose of keeping out of service. . . . [30]

If General Jackson was uncertain as to whether the Mennonites and Dunkers were sincere in their claims for religious objection to war on March 21, 1862, when he wrote to Governor Letcher's aide-de-camp, he was apparently convinced very soon after this time. On March 31, 1862, an order was issued by Jackson to Lieutenant Colonel J. R. Jones who commanded the 33rd Volunteer Regiment to have all the militia men of Rockingham to report to the county courthouse on Thursday morning, April 4. In relaying the order Lieutenant Colonel Jones stated: "I am authorized to say to the Tunkers and Mennonites, that General Jackson believes them to be sincere in their opposition to engaging in war and will detail them as teamsters. . . . They can serve their state as well in such capacity as if bearing arms." [31]

General Jackson's plan to organize these men "into companies of one hundred men each" suggests that the total of Mennonite, Dunker, and Quaker objectors was considerable by the early months of 1862. Already by the summer of 1861 Rockingham was reported to have had 2,700 soldiers in the field. [32]

No reply from General Jackson to Governor Letcher has been found, although such a reply was promptly made, for on March 31, 1862, General Jackson again writes to Colonel French as follows: "I will see that the religionists who are opposed to fighting but consent to serve as teamsters have their pay secured." [33]

Most of the men seem to have entered into the militia service in July, 1861. It was early in this same month that there appeared in the Rockingham *Register* a lengthy article addressed specifically *To the Tunkers, Mennonites and Others Opposed to War,* commending them "for their orderly and honest lives and for that industry and attention to their own business that contributes most to the material interests of a community." The writer of the article then proceeds to justify Southern resistance and to prove that the Union was the aggressor, while the South fought merely in self-defense. He argued that in this situation the Christian can only support his government and from this premise states that nonresistance demands "that one ought . . . to go twice the length demanded, that if the government drafts one of your sons in the militia, you ought to send another as a volunteer." In more direct language, the writer argued:

> There is no compulsion upon you to anybody when you go to war; but you can take your choice of making yourself a target at which the enemy may shoot, and thus carry out your nonresistance principles fully or you may defend yourself against them. The battlefield will be one of the very best stages on which to exhibit your deep conviction that all resistance is wrong. [34]

That this letter was read with considerable apprehension is evident from the reaction of the Dunker leadership. Elder John Kline upon seeing it "sent it to Elder B. F. Moomaw with a request that he should meet it in defense of the principles of peace." A reply was sent to the *Register* but its publication was refused. [35] However, an anonymous reply was published which defended the Tunkers and Mennonites and described their religious scruples about war as "part and parcel of the very foundation . . . of the faith" which they "will seal . . . with their blood rather than fight with the carnal weapons of warfare." [36]

In the autumn of 1861 many of the men in the militia from Rockingham County who were encamped near Winchester were returned to their homes. Most of these "came from Mount Jackson on foot, and were pretty fagged down by the time they got within striking distance of home. They began to get into town pretty early in the afternoon, some of the poor fellows pressing on to their homes without waiting for their formal discharge from their officers who were lingering behind to bring up the rear." [37] Apparently these men were allowed to return to help with the fall planting, with the understanding that they would return to service.

Presumably there were among this returning group some Mennonites and Dunkers. [38] Members of these groups for the most part apparently refused to return to service. They were encouraged in this stand by the Mennonite Bishop Samuel Coffman who held that those who responded to military service disqualified

themselves for church membership.[39]   Daniel Heatwole, a young Mennonite minister, stated some years
after the war that any Mennonites who took part in
the rebellion voluntarily were expelled from the
church.[40]   L. J. Heatwole recalled when "a brother
made public confession for military service." Only a
"few brethren volunteered . . . but they were held
under censure for doing so." [41]

Records are scant on the experience of men detailed to work as teamsters and other work not directly concerned with military action. The writer did locate
a petition to Governor Letcher for the detail of five
men, four of whom were probably Mennonites or from
Mennonite families. These five men were detailed to
help furnish nitre to the Confederate government.[42]
Samuel Brunk was detailed to work on the Baltimore
Railroad.[43]   Joseph E. Niswander (Nieswander) was
detailed to work at shoemaking in the neighborhood.[44]
Henry L. Rhodes was detailed to driving a team.[45]

The practice of securing a substitute to evade military service was common in the Confederacy as it was
in the Union. As early as the autumn of 1861 the Confederate War Department permitted release for volunteers who presented able-bodied proxies. The eventual
1862 conscription act sanctioned the practice. A conscript, under this law, might take a substitute with him
when he was summoned, and if the proxy was healthy
and not subject to service on his own account, the conscript could return home. In 1862 and 1863 newspapers
carried bids for the service of substitutes ranging from

five hundred dollars in 1862 to several thousand dollars in late 1863. [46] On December 28, 1863, Congress abolished the substitute system. [47]

The securing of substitutes was not uncommon among the Mennonites. Peter Blosser furnished a substitute, namely, Daniel J. Coakley, in 1861, to whom he paid only fifteen dollars a month. However, Coakley served only one and one-half months after which Blosser himself was taken into the militia. [48] Jacob Geil secured a substitute for six months and paid him six hundred dollars. After the expiration of this time his substitute returned and Geil was again notified to report for service. However, he was able to evade service by buying out the postmaster position at Edom for two hundred dollars, accepting this position as the lesser of two evils until the exemption law was passed after which he paid the fine and sold the postmastership for five hundred dollars. [49] Abraham Blosser purchased a mail route from a lame Methodist preacher, George W. Stanly, in July, 1861, for one thousand dollars on the same day a call "was issued for every able-bodied man to be pressed into the Confederate army." The reaction caused by a sound man securing exemption by taking a lame man's place prompted Blosser to apply for another route in addition. This was arranged and the community reaction subsided. Blosser carried mail for nearly four years. [50] George Brunk hired a substitute from Page County for twelve months by the name of Bray, and paid him fifty dollars a month. [51] Joseph Beery urged a substitute secured for his son to desert the Confederate service. The substitute reported Beery's disloyalty and Beery was arrested and imprisoned. [52]   Henry L. Rhodes had a substitute furnished by his employer. [53]   John Brunk sent a substitute in the place of a son.[54] Others   who secured substitutes were David C. Breneman, Henry Geil, John Geil, Jacob Shank, Jr., Samuel Shank, and Isaac Wenger. [55]

Although Mennonites and Dunkers generally took advantage of the opportunity to secure substitutes, the Quakers were reluctant to do this.

Chapter *4*

FUGITIVES AND DESERTERS

With the opening up of the late 1862 spring campaign the pressure to obtain every able-bodied man increased. By this time the church had developed a clearer conception of its proper attitude in the situation, firmly recommending refusal to respond to the call. This firm stand encouraged the majority of men to take an attitude of noncooperation in contrast to the cooperative attitude of 1861. Many more men than heretofore hid or fled.

The political transition involving the western counties of Virginia placed the Shenandoah Valley adjacent to an area which, although claimed by Virginia, was actually in the process of becoming Union territory. This circumstance presented the harassed groups with religious scruples against war participation with the real prospect of hiding and flight into and beyond the mountain ranges that comprised the area west of the Valley.

By 1862 an extensive system of hideouts and escape

routes was already developed and was commonly referred to as the "Underground Railroad." Numerous homes which were favorably situated near the mountains were used to conceal refugees and deserters. Weavers Church was also utilized as a hiding place.[1]   The men who were reluctant to attempt to escape over the mountains either out of fear of being apprehended or because of reluctance to leave their families, hid themselves in the nearby mountains or in secret places at their homes or at the homes of others.[2]   These hiding places were called depots, a term which meant that persons opposed to the war, who were anxious to desert the Confederacy, stayed here until the guides, called pilots, who would take them through the mountains, had arrived in the adjacent mountain vicinity. The men who were hoping to escape stayed at these homes for periods of several days to several weeks. The best descriptions of homes that served as depots are in the testimonies of persons who presented claims to the Civil War Claims Commission. The writer lists below the various individual cases of testimony concerning their participation in the system.

> John Brunk—Aided deserters and refugees in escaping. Hid them at his home and fed them. Had charge of Weaver's Church near his home where he also hid men.[3]
>
> Jacob Geil—Helped deserters and refugees to escape. Some names mentioned. Fed and harbored them. Cared for several families. Assisted families of deserters to get away also.[4]

Daniel J. Good—Aided and encouraged deserters and refugees to escape by keeping them at his home, including three soldiers from Jackson's army.[5]

Daniel P. Good—Frequently harbored and kept refugees at his house. Some stayed two or three weeks at a time. Gives numerous names. Helped 75 to 100 men.[6]

Henry L. Rhodes—Put several persons on route of Underground Railroad who were liable for military service. Some names mentioned. Gave money to refugees to enable them to get through. Brought refugees and deserters to his house and helped them escape.[7]

John Rhodes—Harbored, fed, and concealed deserters and refugees at his place. Encouraged them to escape, telling them where to go. Always knew when a party was going through the mountains.[8]

Margaret Rhodes—Aided persons to escape. Many came and stayed at her place, five or six at a time. They would stay several days during which time she would prepare their rations after which they would start off at night. Had a place under floor which was entered by a trapdoor in her bedroom and covered with carpet. Among others, kept Henry Brunk who stayed for a long period because of the condition of his wife and family nearby. After his wife recovered he went through the mountains.[9]

Jacob Wenger—Kept men concealed at his place. Fed them and sent them by guides to mountains. He and his wife carried young John Beery about ten miles in a carry-all to get him within Union lines. Names of other individuals mentioned.[10]

Although no detailed description is given, the home of David Hartman was also a depot which was located

only about a mile from the Daniel P. Good home. 11
Other persons whose homes were not necessarily recog-
nized as depots, but who aided refugees, were Samuel
Shank, Joseph Beery, Samuel Coffman, and George
Brunk. 12

Some of the refugees and deserters themselves have
left testimony concerning help received. Gabriel D.
Heatwole tells of the help given to his brothers by
Daniel J. Good. Peter Wenger and Simon Burkholder
also testify concerning the help received from Good in
concealing them until they could take flight through the
mountains. 13

The families operating the depots usually were informed when a party was to take off through the mountains.[14]   Guides would come to the depots or to other
designated points and take the refugees and deserters
to the mountains by night where the pilots would
conduct them through Union lines. 15   Levi A. Wenger,
a Dunker deserter of January, 1864, tells of being
directed to John Riley, a pilot who called the group
of nineteen refugees "in line and demanded a fee of
twenty dollars apiece in Confederate money, and being
assured that we were all true men, he gave us instructions, and we followed him on foot across a rugged
mountain" to Riley's home for the night after which he
"started with us again, travelling hard all day through
bushy mountains and ravines, a distance of twenty miles.
The next day he turned us over to another pilot by the
name of Leonard Mitchel, who accompanied us to
Petersburg, West Virginia" at which point the group

proceeded under the care of Union soldiers. [16] Apparently the timing of the trips to the mountains to meet the pilots did not always work perfectly. John Brunk tells of one occasion when he accompanied a party of four refugees, one of whom was a second time deserter, several miles to a place appointed to meet their guide. The guide met them but informed them that the mountain pilots were not ready. [17] Daniel J. Good described the "Underground Railroad" as having depots where the refugees and deserters would meet just before the "train" would start. After the "train" started, others would join at other places. [18]

The elaborateness of the whole enterprise was further demonstrated by the system of letter delivery. One of the well-recognized "postmasters" of the "Underground Railroad" was Margaret H. Rhodes, wife of Henry H. Rhodes, who died in July, 1864. Escaped refugees would write back to their friends and send the letters to her care. The guides would bring them back to her and she would distribute them. Mrs. Rhodes at the same time would receive letters to send back with the guides. Sometimes she traveled a distance of six miles by herself to deliver letters, leaving her five children with her mother-in-law. [19] Henry L. Rhodes also carried letters and sent and received them through the lines. [20]

This work of aiding refugees and deserters was of the most dangerous type. Confederate officials were always on the lookout for such disloyal activities. The fact that relatively few persons were known to be held for such activities suggests the effectiveness of the secrecy surrounding the entire enterprise. However, there were some frightening episodes.

John Rhodes was called out one night by a party that posed as Yankees, dressed in blue clothing. This happened soon after he had sent his son John J. Rhodes north with some refugees. Rhodes recognized the party as being comprised of secessionists. They questioned him about his son and concerning other matters, but apparently little more was done. [21]

Jacob Geil was suspected of helping refugees and was closely watched. His home was said to be a "Union hole." On one occasion a party came to his home at night with orders to arrest him and his father, John Geil. The visitors posed as refugees desiring assistance in getting through the lines, but Geil thwarted their scheme by suspecting their motives and thus preventing the arrests. [22]

Chaper *5*

FLIGHT AND PRISON

The spring of 1862 held special significance for the Shenandoah Valley. General Thomas J. Jackson, known as Stonewall Jackson since the First Battle of Manassas, had been given the command of the District of the Shenandoah in October, 1861, by the newly appointed commander of the Department of Northern Virginia, Joseph E. Johnston. Jackson's headquarters were established at Winchester.

When Jackson learned that Union troops were leaving Western Virginia to join McClellan in the Peninsular Campaign, he began a series of actions aimed at preventing such strengthening of McClellan's might. These actions comprise the 1862 Valley Campaign, the main part of which lasted only three weeks, from May 19 to June 9. During this time Jackson and his men marched 170 miles with accumulating enemy stores and prisoners, fought off, eluded, or defeated segments of Union forces totaling upward of 50,000 converging on them from three directions. [1]

This direct involvement of the Valley in this military action greatly agitated the communities in which Mennonite peoples lived. The Valley churches in these times were led by John Geil in the Northern District, Samuel Coffman in the Middle, and Jacob Hildebrand in the Southern. Apparently all stood firm in opposing military service. Outstanding in this respect was Samuel Coffman, who was ordained bishop in 1861 at 39 years of age to replace Martin Burkholder who died in December, 1860.[2]

During this period of political transition when West Virginia was emerging, scouts of both the North and South combed the mountains for deserters. Augusta, Rockingham, and Shenandoah counties remained Virginia counties, while Hardy and Pendleton counties were incorporated into the newly formed Union state.

A half day's walking from the northeastern extremity of Rockingham County would bring one to the vicinity of Petersburg in Hardy County, which at times was occupied by Union forces. The people in this general area were well acquainted with some of the people in the Shenandoah Valley.[3] The Dunkers had established churches there before the war[4] and the Mennonites carried on preaching there as well.[5] It was quite common for relatives or friends to go there to visit or to obtain employment. Once at Keyser, West Virginia, or Oakland, Maryland, it was not far to Ohio and the West via the Baltimore and Ohio Railroad.[6] (See page 49.)

When flight was undertaken, the tendency was to

*Section of Official
Topographical Map*

This is a section of a
photograph of Plate
CXXXVII, General
Topographical Map,
Sheet II in the *Atlas* to
*Accompany the Official
Records of the Union and
Confederate Armies*, pub-
lished under the direction
of the Secretaries of War
from 1891 to 1895 as a
series of separate folders
and later issued as two
volumes.

49

flee in groups, utilizing the services of the mountain guides who served in the "Underground Railroad." This study will concern itself mainly with two groups about which considerable records are in existence. However, there were other groups. Henry L. Rhodes tells of starting north in a group of fourteen behind the party of "seventy who were captured." Fearing to proceed farther, this party also hid in the mountains "until the fine law was passed." [7]   D. H. Zigler, the Brethren (Dunker) historian, tells of a company of eight which got as far as Pendleton County which was then being raided by the Confederates, forcing them to go to the mountains for safety where they were forced to remain for some time. [8]   Whether any Mennonites were included in this group is not known. However, the close cooperation between these two very similar groups (Mennonites and Dunkers) during these war years makes it quite likely that Mennonites were included. [9]   Levi Wenger and his brother M. H. Wenger, both Dunkers, fled north in January, 1864. This group of nineteen stopped off at Jacob Shank's (a Mennonite). By the time they left Petersburg, West Virginia, the group comprised sixty-three members. Still other small groups were formed. [10]

I. THE SEVENTY-FOUR

The larger of the two groups, and the one about which considerable information is available, is the one frequently referred to as the "seventy." Actually this group seems to have been comprised of seventy-six men by the time Petersburg was reached. Two men escaped en route to Staunton[11] and seventy-four reached Richmond. [12]

P. S. Hartman implies that this group was mostly Mennonite. [13] This does not agree with the statement of Simeon Heatwole, certainly a more reliable source, since Heatwole himself was one of the group, and also a Mennonite. Heatwole claimed that there were nearly as many Mennonites as Dunkers and lists sixteen names, ten of which were members of the family of Gabriel Heatwole, Sr. Six others are listed and definitely identified as Mennonite men. Apparently all of the members of the Gabriel Heatwole family, of which he was one, were Mennonite, although he does not say so. [14]

In early March [15] this larger group of fugitives headed over Shenandoah Mountain and traveled until they reached the South Branch of the Potomac at Petersburg.[16] Crossing the river into Petersburg under the gaze of many of the town's residents, [17] they proceeded on their flight until captured by two Confederate scouts a short distance beyond Petersburg. Taken back to Petersburg where they were searched, the captives were soon started on their long march over the mountains toward imprisonment in Richmond. [18] Failing to reach Franklin by nightfall, they stopped for the night at the home of a Captain Bond on the North Mill Creek, where Peter Blosser, a Mennonite, managed to escape from the group. [19]

At Franklin several additional captives were added to the group. Here they were all placed in the courthouse to sleep on the floor under guard. The following day Monterey was reached and the next two days were spent en route to Staunton during which David Miller, a Dunker member of the group, escaped.[20]

Simeon Heatwole describes the two days from Monterey to Staunton as a "wearisome journey across narrow valleys, over ridges and rough mountains."[21] The group arrived at Staunton about 2:00 p.m. on a Wednesday, and were placed in the courthouse, the doors and windows of which were each guarded by a sentinel.[22]   Here they were given plenty to eat. Here too their horses were taken and put into service. The next morning they were placed on the train and traveled on the Central Railroad of Virginia all that day and into the following night.[23]

On the night of their arrival in Richmond they were placed together in a large room which Simeon Heatwole described as having "no accommodations whatever. When we lay down on the floor for the night, the floor was nearly covered and when provisions were brought to us they were generally in buckets."[24]   Joseph A. Miller, describing this as the worst night of the trip, states that they stayed in unheated quarters on a cool night with no bedding or other provisions. Some of the men walked the room nearly all night.[25]

However, these quarters were only temporary, for the next day they "were moved to a more comfortable house and furnished with bedding and provisions."[26]   These quarters have been referred to by Mennonite writers as Libby Prison. This conclusion was easy to make since the building was in the same general vicinity as the very famous Libby Prison. However, a careful check into the practice of the Confederate placing of prisoners and the information produced by the Richmond Civil War Centennial Committee as well as the claims of some writers all seem to prove that the place was not actually Libby Prison but Castle Thunder. [27]   E. Merton Coulter describes Castle Thunder as the best-known Confederate prison for political prisoners and soon there was merged with it another, Castle Lightning. [28]

The group imprisoned at Castle Thunder were treated "considerately by the guards and prison officials." [29] Letters were allowed to be sent and received. Union prisoners who stayed in another room on the same floor were friendly to the men and "were sorry to see us leave the building when we got our liberty." John Hopkins, member of the Virginia House of Delegates from Rockingham County, visited the men in prison and promised to help them. [30]

While awaiting the pleasure of the military authorities the group was examined by S. S. Baxter, of the War Department. Two reports were issued by Baxter, one of which apparently has not been used previously by writers on the subject. This is dated March 28, 1862, and is described as a report "of persons examined who are willing to volunteer" and who are recommended to be placed in regiments. This report includes twenty-seven names from the group of seventy who wished to go into "Stonewall" Jackson's brigade. Among this group are listed such names as J. Showalter, Jacob

Nieswander, Manasses Heatwole, Henry M. Wanger (Wenger), Rush Rhodes, Isaac Suter, and Jacob Wanger (Wenger). [31]

Three days later another report was issued concerning forty-five "persons whose religion forbids shedding blood." Attached to this report is a notation concerning two additional names. The forty-five are described as "members in good standing in the Tunker and Mennonite churches." [32]

It is apparent that the twenty-seven who were willing to volunteer consisted of non-church members who were not eligible to request exemption on the basis of religious objection to military service.

Joseph A. Miller, one of the group, described an interview with Baxter as follows:

> In a day or two twelve of us were taken before Judge Baxter, and he said, "Gentlemen, I will ask you a good many questions, and if I ask any that you cannot answer, you need not say anything." He then asked many questions concerning what we had been doing during the war, and whether we had been in the service. He also asked us whether we had fed the soldiers and their families. We answered all his questions save one, and the judge was kind enough to answer that for us; which was, "Would you feed the enemy, should he come to your house?" He said, "We are commanded to feed our enemies." This was a correct answer. Before dismissing us the judge said we would be sent home soon to work on our farms. [33]

How long was the group kept at Richmond? Some

Castle Thunder

In this building the seventy-four who were taken to Richmond were imprisoned. Constructed of brick, it was described by one of the group as an old tobacco warehouse with windows securely barred.

E. Merton Coulter, a leading historian of the Confederacy, described the building as the best-known Confederate prison for political prisoners. This building is not to be associated with Libby Prison which was only for officers. (Photograph secured through courtesy of City of Richmond Civil War Centennial Commission.)

sources give six weeks as the length of time involved. 34
However, none of these sources are directly from persons who were actually in the group. Joseph A. Miller,
a member of the imprisoned group, states: "We were
in Richmond thirty days," and "We were absent from
home in all thirty-seven days." 35 · This appears to be
the most accurate account of the time involved.

II. THE EIGHTEEN

The other group of fugitives about which detailed
information is available is the so-called group of
"twenty," which consisted of only eighteen. 36   Only
several Mennonites were included in the group, most
of the others being Dunkers. Sometime in March,
likely very soon after the larger group was arrested,
this group also was arrested by Confederate pickets as
it approached Moorefield in Pendleton County. One
or two of the party escaped at this time. The captured
group was taken back to the pickets camp, stripped of
money and other valuable possessions, including $6,000
in gold and silver and eighteen fine horses, 37   and
placed in a room where "we had worship before we
retired" and "prayed for our release and our captors"
after which we slept "on the floor with our budgets
for a pillow." The next day they traveled over the
mountains to Woodstock, the men riding on their own
horses which were taken from them here. The group
was then marched southward to Mount Jackson where
they stayed for some days. 38

Finally they were marched to Harrisonburg where

*The Rockingham County Courthouse as It
Appeared During the Civil War*

This building which was constructed in 1833 replaced the
old 1784 structure. It was replaced in 1874. Here the group
of eighteen fugitives were imprisoned in 1862. Their number
was enlarged by the arrest of two Mennonite ministers, Gabriel
Heatwole, Sr., and Joseph Beery, and Dunker Elder John
Kline. (Photo secured through courtesy of Rockingham Public
Library.)

they were placed in the large jury room on the second floor of the Rockingham County Courthouse. While here they were put to work loading and unloading wagons. Their stay at Harrisonburg was probably shorter than was the stay of the group at Richmond. [39]

This group was eventually enlarged by the addition of Gabriel Heatwole, Sr., Joseph Beery, and John Kline, all church leaders, the first two Mennonite ministers and the last-named a prominent Dunker elder. The newspaper description of the arrest of these church leaders shows evidence of real suspicions on the part of local officials. Apparently these church leaders were being closely watched and at the time Jackson's army was encamped at Mount Jackson after his defeat at Kerns-town on March 23, these men were suddenly arrested and imprisoned with the arrested deserters in the county courthouse. [40]   The newspaper account de-scribes these men as being suspected of "pro-Union proclivities" and "as always having sustained good characters, but . . . as strong Union men" who were "elderly gentlemen, men of property and have there-fore exercised considerable influence in the spheres in which they moved." No formal charges, however, were placed against them. [41]

They were arrested on Saturday, April 5, on which day a damp rainy spell of weather commenced which continued interspersed with snow for three days making the room where they stayed very uncomfortable. On Sunday, April 6, Elder Kline preached on the subject of "Righteousness, Temperance and a Judgement to Come." Kline writes, "I aimed at comforting my brother captives and myself with the recollection that Paul was once a captive like ourselves and that in this state of imprisonment he preached upon the text which I have selected for this day."[42]

By Wednesday, April 9, the "minds and spirits of nearly all of the prisoners are so broken down by their state and prospects of the country that interesting and instructive conversations can hardly be held." Sickness struck the men early in their stay, while the dampness in the room and the lack of comfortable bedding and the lack of fuel added to their distress. Elder Kline contracted a severe cold which made him hoarse. [43] His presence with the imprisoned group was deeply appreciated, however, not only by the Dunker men, but by the Mennonite men as well. Henry Niswander, one of the Mennonite men, commented in later years, "If Timothy loved Paul more than I loved Brother Kline, his love was great." Kline not only preached but also served as a physician to their physical needs. [44] The sentiment of the imprisoned group is probably best expressed by "The Prisoner's Song." Composed at Mount Jackson by the group of eighteen prisoners, the chorus was added by Elder John Kline when they were all imprisoned in Harrisonburg. [45]

This group was not treated as considerately by the guards and prison officials as was the larger group at Richmond. [46] One night when one of the prisoners was standing at a window a shot was sent through

the window, narrowly missing the young man. [47]
The plight of this group, however, was relieved by the
ministrations of women from home communities who
brought baskets of provisions for the men. [48]

While in prison John Kline wrote a reply to an
article published in the April 11, 1862, issue of the
Rockingham *Register* which insinuated that the three
arrested men had used their influence against the
Confederacy. Apparently Kline's letter was not published. [49] The newspaper was forced to suspend
operations when the Union army took possession a
few days later. [50]

The less humane treatment received by the group
imprisoned in Harrisonburg in contrast to the group
imprisoned in Richmond seems to indicate the existence of a pronounced resentment on the part of some
of the local population. This resentment was apparently intensified by the excitement and agitation created
by the push of the Union army up the Valley. After
Jackson's defeat at Kernstown on March 23, he drew
back to Mount Jackson where he remained until the
middle of April, all the while recruiting his forces and
reorganizing his regiments. Jackson then retired to
Harrisonburg where he turned eastward and located
at Swift Run Gap on April 20, at which place he
remained until May 1.

General Nathaniel Banks meanwhile camped his
Union army in the vicinity of Harrisonburg. Hartman
describes Banks' soldiers as well disciplined, paying
for the produce they secured and fraternizing with

the farmers. He states that Union soldiers "would come to our house, sit down, and talk and get us to sing for them." [51]

Chapter 6

STRUGGLES
FOR RECOGNITION

The families of the captured men eventually heard of their capture and became fearful that their fathers, brothers, husbands, and sons would be executed. Today, this exaggerated sense of fearfulness is difficult to realize in light of the unusually high rate of desertion which we now know took place. However, although in actual practice the punishment for desertion was seldom in proportion to the gravity of the offense, the death sentence was carried out sufficiently to impress the public.[1]   In August, 1862, two soldiers from Rockingham were ordered shot by Jackson for desertion[2]   and in December, 1863, William A. Coffman of Rockingham County was tried by court-martial and "charged with piloting and assisting deserters from the Confederate army to escape to the enemy's lines and with communicating information to the enemy's country." He was sentenced to death by hanging.[3]

Mennonites and Dunkers were under suspicion of

assisting deserters in escaping and the capture of a group in the act of desertion itself could well have given the Confederate authorities a good opportunity to effect some impressive punishment. At any rate, these weeks were "a serious and solemn time in which earnest and genuine supplication was made to God for help." The members of the Mennonite congregations were called together and through consultation it was decided to contact legislative officials. [4]

In spite of a certain degree of unfavorable sentiment against the Mennonites and Dunkers and in spite of the suspicions of disloyalty to the Confederate cause on the part of many civilians and the military, a substantial reservoir of local goodwill was also present. This reservoir of goodwill was put under a severe strain in 1862 as the local population became aware of the arrest of the separate groups of deserters and of several church leaders. Add to this strain the general fear and emotion generated by the Union push up the Valley, and one can readily comprehend the tendency of public feeling to work to the disadvantage of those who were opposed to military service.

Apparently, as in 1861, accusations were still forthcoming which insinuated that the Valley residents tended to be disloyal.[5] In Virginia and the Confederacy at large the concept that disloyalty was characteristic of the Valley was encouraged by the development of what was known as the "Blue Ridge Rebellion." This uprising "embraced . . . at one time between three hundred and four hundred persons from sixteen to over forty-five years of age." The group consisted of natives of not only Rockingham, but also Greene and Page counties with a few from Albemarle County. 6

The courage of young Bishop Samuel Coffman stands out in striking fashion when one appreciates these conditions in the Valley in early 1862. In uncompromising fashion he encouraged those pressed into service to take a firm stand, holding that those who responded were disqualifying themselves for membership in the church. Coffman was not urging such a course from a position of personal immunity from molestation, for he himself received criticism from the public and eventually threats were made on his life. A Confederate military official threatened to come with his regiment and take Coffman and all his members of military age. The seriousness of the threats is evident from the fact that he decided to go North for a time until the bitter sentiment against him would subside. He left Virginia in May, 1862, and spent six weeks in the North during which time he preached in the churches of Maryland and Pennsylvania.7

Through all of these experiences, the faith of these people was put under additional strain because of sickness, especially diphtheria. In the spring of 1862 a very serious epidemic of diphtheria swept through .the Valley causing many deaths, especially among the young. John Kline was kept very busy ministering to the sick.8   In the late summer the epidemic was still serious, for John Kline entered the following into his journal on September 7, 1862: "Diphtheria is raging. It almost rivals the sword in its destruction of life. The sword cuts down the men in middle life and diphtheria cuts down the children." [9]   The epidemic continued through autumn and winter. [10]

I. VIRGINIA PROVIDES EXEMPTION

Early in the war period correspondence in the interests of securing recognition for religious objectors was carried on with government officials, especially state officials. There is considerable evidence that contacts with government officials were made by Dunker and Quaker leaders. There seems to be no specific evidence of similar Mennonite attempts in the earlier period. I will not deal with the Quaker efforts which are amply dealt with by Edward Needles Wright in his excellent work, *Conscientious Objectors in the Civil War.* [11]   However, I am including the main efforts made by Dunker leaders because it is my impression that the Dunker leaders were more forthright in their efforts than the Mennonites and also because of the fact that by the spring of 1862, if not before, the Dunkers and Mennonites worked together to some degree. [12]

On January 30, 1861, John Kline wrote to commend Governor John Letcher for his stand for the Union and pleaded that the Dunkers be spared from military service if war developed. The governor replied courteously, stating: "I think it entirely reasonable that

Bishop Samuel Coffman
(1822-1894)

Coffman united with the Mennonite Church in 1848 and in 1852 was ordained to the ministry. On May 11, 1861, he was ordained to the office of bishop at the age of 39. Coffman took a firm stand in opposition to military service during the Civil War. (Photo through courtesy of Nellie Coffman.)

those who have conscientious scruples in regard to the performance of military duty should be relieved by the payment of a small pecuniary compensation." [13]

As soon as militia units were pressed into service, state officials were visited and military officials written to and visited in person by Dunker leaders and at least in one instance by a lay member. [14] Numerous Dunker leaders were involved, but none were as active in this regard as John Kline. On February 1, 1861, he wrote to John T. Harris, the local Representative in the United States Congress before the war, who was a personal friend of Kline's, beseeching him "to do all he can to avert the calamity that now threatens us. . . ." [15] On July 22, 1861, in another letter to Governor Letcher he wrote:

> It seems to me that the proceedings of some of our officers is [sic] entirely too rash. Many men in our parts who are absolutely not proper subjects for field or soldier service, are not exempted, who might soon give out in a soldier's life, while at home, with fine care to themselves they might be useful and do considerable service. Others who have small families and (wives) who are in a state of utrogestation, expecting to go to bed in a few weeks or (month), it seems that in such cases it is cruel to take away the husband from them. Other cases have been that men conscientious of bearing arms were bound, and forced, to go against the feeling of their faith, and the solemn vow that they have made to their God, to be true to the doctrine of the Saviour and Prince of Peace, who declares that they "who would be his disciples must deny

themselves, take up their cross, and follow him (daily)."[16]

In December, 1861, Kline wrote to John Hopkins and John C. Woodson—both members of the Virginia House of Delegates—and to Charles H. Lewis, a Confederate officer, entreating them to stand in defense of the Tunkers and explicitly explaining the reasons for refusing to bear arms, entreating them to devise some plan by which they could be exempted. [17] In the letter to Colonel Lewis he states:

> . . . The privilege usually granted Christian people to pay a fine has been overruled and set aside, and they are compelled to take up weapons of carnal warfare to drill and if need be to shoot down their fellowman. This is without precedent in a land of Christian liberty. . . . This state of things the much abused Abe Lincoln would have much deplored. For I am credibly informed that he issued a proclamation that no conscientious Christian should be forced to war or to take up arms.
>
> Please give this matter your earnest attention and tell it or read it to your fellow officers, and if expedient to General Jackson.

Colonel Lewis replied sympathetically to this straight-forward letter. [18]   Late in December, Kline wrote again to Colonel Lewis and also to General Jackson himself. In February, 1862, he wrote to Governor Letcher, again to Colonel Lewis, and also to Confederate Secretary of War, Judah Benjamin. [19]

Other influences were also brought to bear on the Virginia General Assembly, especially through delegates

from the Valley counties such as Delegate George
Baylor of Botetourt County where numerous Dunkers
lived and Delegates Algernon Gray and John Hopkins of Rockingham County. [20]

Another Dunker who led out in contacting officials
was Elder B. F. Moomaw from Botetourt County who
had demonstrated consistent courage in the secession
crisis in his home community. He personally visited
Delegate George Baylor and secured his interest in
supporting a petition drawn up by the Dunkers and
Mennonites. [21] This petition was given attention by
the House of Delegates and on March 24 Representative Charles Gratton moved that the "committee
for courts of justice enquire into the expediency of
fixing a commutation to be paid by those persons whose
religious tenets forbid them bearing arms." On March
25 Representative John C. Rutherford from Gooch-
land introduced from the Committee for the Courts
of Justice a bill to "exempt certain parties upon
religious grants." This bill was taken up on motion of
Representative John H. Hopkins on March 27 who
then submitted by way of amendment a substitute
for the bill which was in due course voted on and
passed 79 to 18. [22] Amendments by the Senate
proposed the paying of a lump sum plus a tax on
property and requiring persons liable for militia
duty and unable to make such payment, to serve as
teamsters or in some other service not involving the
bearing of arms.[23] After the House agreed to these
Senate amendments, the bill became law on March

29, 1862. Section I provided:

> . . . that whenever upon application for exemption
> to the board of exemption, it shall appear to said
> board that the party applying for said exemption
> is bona fide prevented from bearing arms, by the
> tenets of the church to which said applicant belongs,
> and did actually belong at the passage of this act,
> and further, that said applicant has paid to the
> sheriff of the county or collector of taxes for the
> city or town in which said applicant resides, the sum
> of five hundred dollars, and in addition thereto,
> the further sum of two per cent of the assessed value
> of said applicant's property, then the said board, on
> the presentation of the receipt of said officers for
> said moneys, and after the said applicant shall have
> taken an oath or affirmation that he will sustain
> the confederate government, then the said board shall
> exempt the said applicant: provided, that whenever
> said party may be unable, or shall fail to pay the
> said sum of five hundred dollars, and the tax of
> two per centum on their property, he shall be
> employed (when liable to militia duty) in the ca-
> pacity of teamster, or in such other character as
> the service may need, which does not require the
> actual bearing of arms: and provided further, that
> the persons so exempted do surrender to the board
> of exemption all arms which they may own, to be
> held subject to the order of the governor, for public
> use. [24]

The Mennonites lost no time in proceeding to
raise the necessary amounts of money and the brother-
hood apparently responded willingly. David Hartman,
father of P. S. Hartman, solicited funds. [25]   Jacob

Geil, a deacon, collected funds also. [26]   The money raised was taken to the appropriate officials to secure the release of the men in prison. Joseph A. Miller points out that soon after this time a good horse sold for a thousand dollars which paid two fines. [27]   L. J. Heatwole claims that Emmanuel Suter was delegated to carry the necessary funds to Richmond for the Mennonites in the group. [28]   However, a Mennonite member of the imprisoned group, Simeon Heatwole, states that Benjamin Byerly, who came to visit the group a number of times and preached to them, went around to raise the money and when the fines were paid, accompanied the officers who released the man. [29]   Byerly was a Dunker leader. [30] This corresponds with the testimony of David M. Miller, a Dunker member of the group, who stated that a "Bro. Cline took Augusta Brethren out and Bro. B. F. Byerly took us out who lived in Rockingham." [31]   S. F. Sanger claimed that a committee was sent. [32]   Suter may well have been a member of such a committee.

A quartermaster had visited the imprisoned men in Richmond after they were informed of the passage of the exemption law and endeavored to induce them to enlist as teamsters, but without success. [33]

Some time elapsed before the imprisoned men in both Harrisonburg and Richmond were set free, due to the fact that the fines were not accepted when first offered. [34]   Nair states that many "young men, some with families, continued to flee the country to avoid

both fine and army service and a couple of these
were captured before they could reach the Federal
lines, brought back and lodged in prison." [35.]   Delay
was particularly evident in Harrisonburg, where the
men, including the imprisoned church officials, were
marched northward toward New Market, but on
April 16, when only six miles from that destination,
cannonading was heard to the north, and the group
retraced their route toward Harrisonburg. [36]   Two
of these men had been released on Monday, April
14, and others were apparently released between
that date and Friday, April 18, when the three church
leaders were released without a trial. This was the
day that General Stonewall Jackson and his army
passed through Harrisonburg in his retreat before
Federal troops. [37]   As for the released men from
Richmond, they were sent home on the train as far
as Waynesboro, from which point they proceeded on
foot. [38]

The new legislation was a welcome relief to these
peoples who for more than two years had lived in
great uncertainty. All bona fide church members were
eligible for exemption whether in prison, in military
service, or in hiding. [39]   How many were in military
camps is unknown. Probably most of the men still in
service were not members of the church. It was the
common practice in these times to join church in
late youth or in adult years. This meant that some
men who later became loyal members of the church
were not members at this time and were not eligible

for exemption, the only alternative being military service. Most of these apparently escaped eventually and spent the remaining period of the war either in hiding or as refugees in the North.[40]

The case of Manasses Heatwole belongs in this category. Heatwole was only nineteen years of age in 1862 when he was in the group which was captured and taken to Richmond, but apparently he was not eligible for exemption. [41] Compelled to join the military, he was incorporated into the 52nd Virginia Infantry, Company F, soon deserted, [42] and was apparently inducted again and participated in numerous military engagements, the last of which was the Battle of Gettysburg after which he escaped to Ohio until the war ended. Later he joined the Mennonite Church and "was a faithful and consistent member" until his death.[43]

Another similar case was that of Melchiah Breneman who became a cavalryman, serving in this capacity for over three years. On the day before the Battle of Gettysburg he was wounded, but not fatally. After eight months, before the close of the war, he deserted and with three other men fled north. Breneman settled in Lancaster County, Pennsylvania, until the end of the war, returned to Virginia, and in 1870 moved to Ohio, where he was ordained a deacon of the Mennonite Church. [44]

Henry G. Brunk never secured exemption, for some unkown reason. Brunk apparently was a member of the Mennonite Church. [45] Married just be-

fore the war (1859), Brunk was apprehended with
the group imprisoned in Harrisonburg, [46]   escaped,
and spent two and one-half years in hiding after
which he escaped to the North in a group of seventeen, with David Frank, who was probably not a
church member.[47] Brunk found his way to Illinois. [48]

The case of John D. Heatwole presents a problem
to the historian because of the conflict between tradi-
tional reports and official Civil War records. Tradition-
ally credited with being instrumental in paving the way
for the establishment of Mennonite rural mission work
in what was in the process of becoming West Virginia,
Heatwole entered military service in June, 1861, and
was reported as deserted in the late summer of 1862.
L. J. Heatwole claims that Heatwole successfully
eluded military officials and fled into seclusion in the
mountains where he is claimed to have made his
home till the end of the war.[49]   This account,
however, does not allow for another period of military service. That John D. Heatwole did have another
period of military service is evidenced by the existence of a petition made by ninety-four citizens of
Rockingham County for Heatwole's discharge from the
33rd Virginia Regiment. The War Department received the petition on April 11, 1863, that Heatwole
be discharged to provide their alleged need for a
potter. It is significant that the petition was not made
on the basis of religious objection to military service.
It was denied because the "department has no authority to discharge a soldier for the stated purpose."[50]

II. CONFEDERATE CONSCRIPTION LAW

The great relief experienced by the Mennonites and others who refused military service was only short-lived, for suddenly on April 16, 1862, the control of conscription was placed into the hands of the Confederate government by the passage of a measure which conscripted all men from eighteen to thirty-five for three years of service. This first national conscription law in American history allowed substitutes only under certain conditions and made no provision for religious objectors.[51]

This Confederate law effectually undermined the recent gains which religious objectors had secured and renewed fear and concern especially for those just released. It not only aroused apprehension in Mennonite, Dunker, and Quaker circles but aroused sympathy in some other quarters as well. On June 30, 1862, an article in the *Daily Richmond Whig* stated: "Scattered over certain portions of Virginia are a well-known sect called 'Dunkards.' These Dunkards, in the act of the Legislature calling out militia, were exempted. . . . Under the conscript act which is now being put into operation these men will have to enter the army, no provision being made by Congress for their exemption. It seems hard they should be made to pay and fight too, but as the law now stands there is no help for it." [52]

During the late spring of 1862, after the Virginia exemption measure was voided by the passage

of the Confederate draft law, General Banks
occupied Harrisonburg with about 20,000 men while
General John C. Fremont had charge of another
Union force of 16,000 in the moutains west of the
upper Valley. On May 8 Jackson joined Confeder-
ate General Edward Johnson in a battle against a
Union force at McDowell, pursuing the Union force
to Franklin where Fremont was situated. Jackson
then returned to the Valley via McDowell. Meanwhile
Banks withdrew to Strasburg. Jackson joined up with
General Richard S. Ewell in an attack on Front
Royal, forcing the Union forces to retreat to
Winchester. Here a Union attempt to stop Jackson's
push down the Valley on May 25 was thwarted and
Banks retreated into Maryland as Jackson stormed into
Harpers Ferry and created panic in Washington.

General James Shields was ordered to cross the
Blue Ridge into the Valley while Fremont was
ordered to come east into the Valley. Jackson hastily
pushed up the Valley, arriving in Harrisonburg on
June 5, and again turned eastward, this time to Port
Republic, leaving a large part of his army under
General Ewell at Cross Keys. Meanwhile, on June
6 Fremont occupied Harrisonburg and vicinity. His
soldiers are described as being less considerate of the
local population than were those of Banks. [53]   On
the same day that Fremont arrived in Harrisonburg,
some of his force clashed with a Confederate force two
miles from Harrisonburg, in which encounter Jackson's
cavalry commander, Turner Ashby, was fatally wound-

ed. On Sunday, June 8, occurred the Battle of Cross Keys, an area in which numerous Dunkers and some Mennonites lived. These people took "refuge in their cellars while men were being slaughtered in their golden wheatfields." [54]

During the summer of 1862, Dunker and Mennonite leaders were active once more. This time the exemption again sought for was more difficult to secure than that from the Virginia State Legislature. On April 21, an exemption bill was passed which relieved from military duty, ministers of the Gospel. [55] This measure, if anything, made the Congress less amenable to granting additional exemptions. [56]

Dunker leaders, B. F. Moomaw and Jonas Graybill, personally visited their Representative in Congress urging him to use his influence to secure the help of a Senator. [57] The untiring John Kline wrote to John B. Baldwin of the House of Representatives on July 23, 1862, urging him to "use all your powers and influence in behalf of us, so that the Conscript law or all other Confederate laws be so constructed that Christian conscience be so protected that the south shall not be polluted with a bloody persecution." [58] Baldwin in reply suggested that a petition be drawn up to present to Congress. Kline proceeded to draw up the petition, which included the Dunker and Mennonite churches. This petition was in part as follows:

> The undersigned members of the Tunker and Mennonite Churches in the State of Virginia respectfully

and humbly represent, that at the late Session of the State Legislature of Virginia, that Body passed a law exempting from military duty the members of our Churches, upon each member paying the sum of $500 and two per cent upon all his taxable estate. . . . We appeal to you, to pass a law, ratifying the act of the Legislature of Virginia, on this subject.

It may not be amiss to state here, that under the excitement of the hour, indiscreet, and inconsiderate persons have preferred the charge of disloyalty against our Churches. This charge has not the semblance of truth, in fact, and has doubtless originated from our faith against bearing arms. We would further state, that those of our members embraced in said act of the General Assembly of Virginia have already paid the penalty of $500 and a per cent to the officers of the State, and thus fulfilled our contract, and have complied with the law. We only ask Congress so far to respect our rights, our consciences, and the Act of the State of Virginia, as to ratify the same. . . . [59]

Another petition was circulated in Botetourt, Roanoke, and Franklin counties by the Dunkers which was also presented to Congress through Congressman B. F. Anderson. [60] Other petitions from Quakers and Dunkers were also sent directly to the Congressional Committee on Military Affairs to which all such memorials were eventually referred. [61] On August 26, 1862, Senator William Dortch presented such a memorial of the Quakers of North Carolina to the Senate of the Confederate Congress, asking for exemption from the operation of the conscription law. On September 1, in the House of Representatives, Representative John B. Baldwin "presented a memorial from two religious societies asking the benefit of a certain act of the Virginia legislative in relation to exemptions" which was referred to the Committee on Military Affairs. On September 15, Baldwin again "presented two memorials from members of the Quaker and Dunker religious denominations." [62]   While the Senate considered the above-mentioned bill, Senator Edward Sparrow of Louisiana moved to amend the bill by inserting the words, "all persons who have been and now are members of the Society of Friends and the Association of Dunkers, in regular membership in their respective denomination." [63]   On September 24, the House took this bill under consideration as passed by the Senate which asked not only for an exemption of "certain persons from military duty, but also for a repeal of the April 21, 1852, law." [64] On September 30, Representative Thomas J. Foster of Alabama moved to strike out the words, "and all persons who have been and now are members of the Society of Friends and the Association of Dunkers in regular membership in their respective denominations." Representative Thomas S. Ashe of North Carolina moved to amend by adding: "Provided the members of the Society of Friends or Dunkers shall furnish substitutes or pay a tax of five hundred dollars into the Confederate treasury." Representative Ashe's amendment was agreed to but Representative Foster's amendment was defeated. Representative

William Smith of North Carolina then moved to amend by inserting the word "Mennonists" which was agreed to. [65]   The Committee on Conference to compromise the difference between the Senate and House versions of the bill agreed to recommend the addition of the words "Nazarenes and Mennonists." [66]. The bill became law on October 11, 1862. Section VII which is concerned with religious exemption reads as follows:

> *The Congress of the Confederate States of America do enact,* That all persons who shall be held unfit for military service in the field . . . every minister of religion authorized to preach according to the rules of his sect and in the regular discharge of ministerial duties, and all persons who have been and are now members of the Society of Friends, and the association of Dunkards, Nazarenes, and Mennonists, in regular membership in their respective denominations: *Provided,* Members of the Society of Friends, Nazarenes, Mennonists and Dunkers shall furnish substitutes or pay a tax of five hundred dollars each into the public treasury. . . .
> Approved October 11, 1862. [67]

This new Confederate provision was considerably more liberal than the act previously passed by the Virginia General Assembly. It did not include the two percent on taxable property, nor the demand that qualified persons who could not pay be employed as teamsters or in some other indirect military service.

What prompted the Confederate Congress to adopt such a law? Various explanations have been given. Mennonite sources stress the effect of the Mennonite Confession of Faith translated by Joseph Funk and commonly referred to as the Burkholder Confession of Faith. [68]   L. J. Heatwole states: "The members who at home were called together, after consultation, officials in the Confederate Congress who were acquainted with our people were notified of the real inwardness of the situation and with a copy of our Confession of Faith placed in their hands they moved the Confederate Congress to pass a Bill. . . ." [69] One Dunker writer noted that the Dunkers "had so little literature on their nonresistant principles that it was difficult to establish the faith before the Confederate Congress. . . ." [70]   Abraham Blosser claimed that the Dunkers "had no published discipline or confession of faith, as they say the Bible is their discipline or confession of faith and when our Menonite Confession of Faith was brought into court at Richmond by Algernon S. Gray, Attorney at Law, the Dunkards claimed to hold the same nonresistant doctrine that we do in respect to war." [71]

However, a comment by Samuel Cline, a Dunker from Augusta County to whom Confederate Congressman Baldwin wrote, asking Cline for the "best thing that he had on nonresistance," suggests that the Dunkers may have been influential also. Cline sent Baldwin a copy of W. C. Thurman's pamphlet on *Peace Principles of the Brethren* which was published in that same year. Later Baldwin wrote Cline that "Thurman's pamphlet did the work." [72]

The problem is complicated still more by the claim of Edward Needles Wright that a small pamphlet entitled *Nonresistance, the Patience and the Faith of the Saints* may have been influential on members of Congress. This pamphlet was written by William Thurber, a conscript in the Confederate army who refused to take up arms, was exempted, and afterward published his tract. An editorial in *The Friend*, a Quaker periodical, claimed that "copies were sent to the members of the Richmond Congress, and it is said arguments used had much influence. . . ." [73] It should never be forgotten that the Quakers were always very active in contacting Confederate officials and producing statements on their stand. [74]

Benjamin Funk claims that Algernon S. Gray, who was present when the Confederate Congress passed the exemption law, held "that the capture of the seventy refugees near Petersburg . . . by two individuals, with their quiet submission to authority all the way, did more to impress the members of that Congress than all other influences together." [75]

More important to these groups than the matter of ascertaining the most influential factors was the fact of exemption itself. However, at least one local Confederate official endeavored to collect again from those who had paid for exemption under the now outmoded Virginia measure of March 29. This action prompted the energetic John Kline to write plainly on November 17, on the unreasonableness of this demand, to the official involved. [76]   Very shortly after the passage of the exemption law, the Secretary of War, through the Adjutant Inspector General's office, directed the Quarter master-General at Richmond to select a special Confederate officer to ``receive the sums paid in . . . to secure exemption from military service.''[77]   Before the end of the year the Confederate government had regularized the administration of the law and had designated persons to receive the fines.[78]   In December the Bureau of Conscription was organized, which was given charge of the overall administration of the draft.[79]

The earlier release of the prisoners, the return of the men from hiding and from military service, and now the final passage of a Confederate exemption measure in October produced a deep sense of gratitude on the part of the Mennonites and Dunkers. The Dunkers in Botetourt County through their Elder B. F. Moomaw invited Elder John Kline and the Dunkers of Rockingham and adjacent counties to join them in a public manifestation of gratitude on January 1, 1863.[80] These plans and their observance had their effect on the Mennonites in Virginia. Jacob Hildebrand, Mennonite bishop of the Southern District, influenced by the Brethren precedent, requested that his churches meet together for a similar purpose. The date, January 28, 1863, was agreed to for the occasion. Hildebrand invited Bishop Samuel Coffman of the Middle District and John Geil of the Northern District to join with them. The observance, however, was held as scheduled by the Southern District without the Northern and Middle Districts' participation.[81]

It should be noted by way of contrast that the Quakers were not as well satisfied with the Confederate provision for exemption on the conditions imposed. They expressed appreciation for Congress' good intentions but felt they could not conscientiously pay the tax exacted as the price of religious liberty. Members who could conscientiously avail themselves of the exemption by paying the tax were, however, allowed to do so. [82]   Some of the Quakers also questioned the practice of the payment of war taxes. [83]

Chapter 7

CONTINUED APPREHENSIONS

For the next eighteen months after the granting of exemptions by the Confederate government, the churches had comparative rest. The *Record of Exemptions in Virginia* in the records of the Adjutant and Inspector General's Office includes in the lists fifty-three names of Mennonites.[1]   Although the Confederate Congress experienced pressures to liberalize exemptions for various groups, it did not receive as many petitions from religious objectors in 1863 as it did in 1862.[2]

However, apparently there were influences at work to conscript manpower much more completely than the 1862 measure allowed. On January 22, 1863, the Confederate House of Representatives considered a new exemption bill which was opposed by Representative William Preston of Virginia because its "adoption would place in the hands of the President and the Secretary of War the entire control of every white male inhabitant between the ages of eighteen and forty-five years." Representative Waller Staples of Virginia objected to the bill because it made no provision for substitutes, and because it provided no exemption for certain denominations of Christians. Was "it the purpose of Congress to annul its contract with these men and drag them into the service"? asks the *Richmond Daily Examiner*.[3]   A measure passed on May 1, 1863, repealed clauses of the October, 1862, Act but included no mention of the religious objectors. [4]

Although the Confederate government in general stood by its exemption provisions for religious objectors, it became very hard pressed in the summer of 1863 when the disastrous defeats of Vicksburg and Gettysburg were realized. Governor Letcher called an extra session of the General Assembly. In his message to that body he recommended among other things the abrogation of the exemption of religious objectors. This change of mood on the part of the governor and the expressed sentiment of some of the members of the General Assembly produced deep concern on the part of religious objector groups. In correspondence between Dunker leaders the idea of a petition to leave the country was suggested. [5]   Never before had such a suggestion been indicated.

Meanwhile, on December 7, 1863, President Davis addressed the newly assembled first session of the Congress in which he proposed major changes in conscription legislation in the direction of sparing no effort "to add largely to our effective force as promptly as possible. The sources of supply," he said, "are to be found by restoring to the Army all who are improperly absent, putting an end to substitution, modifying the exemption law, restricting details. . . ." [6]

During the early part of 1863 much discussion occurred in the Confederate Congress on the matter of substitutes. Representative Charles Russell of Virginia held that the practice of substitution had contributed more than anything else to the demoralization and discouragement of the army. [7] Finally, on December 28, 1863, Congress abolished the discredited substitute system. [8]

The Dunkers commissioned Elders B. F. Moomaw and B. F. Byerly to go to Richmond where they contacted members of Congress and returned assuring their people of loyal support in Congress. But news from Richmond indicated that the exemption law was in danger until February, 1864, when word was received from John T. Harris that the "exemption on religious grounds stands firm in Congress." [9] On February 17, 1864, the Confederate Congress had passed the military law which stipulated that "all white men . . . between the ages of seventeen and fifty shall be in the military service of the Confederate States for the war. . . ." More important for this study was the added provision that "no persons heretofore exempted on account of religious opinions, and who has paid the tax levied to relieve him from services, shall be required to render military service under this act." [10] The exemption policy of October 11, 1862, was retained.

There are not enough records preserved to ascertain

whether any appreciable number of persons joined the
Mennonite Church during these years for the purpose
of taking advantage of the religious exemption from
military service. Apparently, in the peace denominations
generally there was this tendency, for John A. Campbell, the Assistant Secretary of War, reported: ". . .
It is understood that a large addition has been made
to these denominations since the enactment of October,
1862, from families not previously connected with them.
This has been a cause for distrust. . . ." [11]   It
should be noted that Campbell was sympathetic to the
religious objectors and did more than any other single
Confederate official to ease their lot. [12]   Brunk states
that it was "reported that Bishop Hildebrand promised to keep some men out of the war if they would
join his church." [13]   Another Mennonite claimed that
the church was thriving, "a great many added . . .
in the last few years, and still more were making
application." [14]   On June 7, 1864, the Confederate
Congress passed an amendment to the February 17,
1864, measure specifying that "the Secretary of War
be . . . authorized to revoke any such exemptions
. . . obtained by fraud, misrepresentation or error." [15]

Neither the October, 1862, provision for the exemption of religious objectors, nor for that matter the
official recommitment to this policy in February, 1864,
quieted all the apprehensions of the Mennonites and
others. Numerous incidents and varied experiences
made them aware that their refusal to place the Confederate cause before their peculiar religious scruples

was being resented by local officials and citizens.

To what extent there was difficulty in getting exemptions for young men who became old enough for military service or for older members when the age limit was extended, this writer has not been able to determine. The increasing number of persons and groups fleeing north seems to indicate difficulty. Levi Wenger, a Dunker minister, tells of his flight with his brother M. H. Wenger. By the time they contacted their pilot their number increased to nineteen. After spending two weeks at Petersburg, the group increased to sixty-three. [16]   Some young men were sent north when at or near military age. [17]   R. J. Heatwole accompanied Henry Brunk with a group of seventeen, fifteen of which "were seventeen-year-old boys." [18]

Mennonite farmers had their teams of horses pressed into service. John Rhodes' team of four horses was pressed to go to Monterey and was kept in use for three months and returned after being worked hard. Later, when Rhodes fed them into good shape, they were taken again and kept. [19]   P. S. Hartman tells of being ordered, when only seventeen years of age, to "hitch up a team and take a load of shoes to Staunton." Arriving at Staunton he saw other neighbors unloading their teams. [20]   David Breneman had horses and wagons impressed and returned. [21]

Peter Blosser had his teams pressed into service at different times to haul stores for the Confederates. Blosser, however, was apparently quite cooperative, for he went along to drive the team, receiving four dollars a day for doing so. The *Summary Report on Blosser's Disallowed Claim* states, "We fail to discover any indications of compulsion in these acts of aid and comfort to the Rebels or any manifestation of suspicion on their part that he was hostile to their cause." [22]

Other unpleasant experiences for Mennonite farmers were the frequent visits of Confederate officers who came in commissary wagons "to haul away corn, wheat, and other provisions, all of which they usually took without leave or license or a cent of pay." [23] Confederate law obligated farmers to pay in kind one tenth of their crops but much in addition was taken. John Brunk had taken from him corn, wheat, hay, and a horse. [24] Daniel P. Good claimed that they took corn, hay, and other things several times, only some of which was paid for. Rather than sell his produce to the Confederates, he sold it to the poor in the community whenever possible. Samuel Coffman had a horse and some grain taken; the grain was paid for but not the horse. John Rhodes also endeavored to sell his produce to the poor rather than allow the Confederates to purchase it. [25] Several articles in the *Register* show that this was general practice for Mennonites and Dunkers. During the early summer of 1863 the Mennonites contributed outright "eleven barrels of flour and a quantity of bacon to the poor and needy families of Confederate soldiers living at the head of Brock's Gap." The article said, "Not a solitary member of this church lived in the region where this timely and generous contribution was made." [26]

In August, 1863, John Kline was again arrested along with Jacob Wine. Taken before the military on August 18 they were released, but six days later they were arrested once more and asked to give an account of themselves and released. [27] In early October Joseph Beery was again arrested along with his son Solomon. They were charged with aiding, advising, and assisting deserters from the Confederate service to escape. The elder Beery was characterized in the newpaper account "as a very determined and uncompromising Union man, and was one of a few men in Rockingham who voted against the Ordinance of Secession." Beery was reported to have been on a visit to the North and returned, "it would seem, to persuade and advise poor, simple, ignorant and foolish people to attempt to abandon their country and her cause and make their way to the lines of the enemy." Beery and son together with Henry May, who was arrested at the same time, were sent to Richmond where they spent four weeks in Castle Thunder waiting for their trial which never was held. Beery and his son were reported to local Confederate officials by the substitute the elder Beery had secured for his son. [28]

Undoubtedly, had the war lasted much longer the difficulties of religious objectors would have increased, for conditions throughout the South deteriorated in these late war years. One major indication of this deterioration in the Shenandoah Valley was the tragic murder of Elder John Kline which occurred on June 15, 1864. Henry Beery testified that at the time of the murder "all Union men were threatened by secessionists and feared violence." [29]   As this writer has attempted to suggest, quite obviously no Dunker or Mennonite leader worked more persistently to secure consideration for religious objectors. Kline had been warned repeatedly by friends of schemes afoot to harm him but he seemed not to develop any sense of fear. [30]   Shortly before his death he said: "I am threatened: they may take my life; but I do not fear them; they can only kill the body." [31] That no effort was made to punish the persons who committed the crime is sheer evidence of the low state of law and order in the Valley in mid-1864.

The increasing violence and lawlessness increased the fear of the peoples in the communities to the extent that public worship services were at times abandoned, the churches holding services in secrecy. [32]   The fear that the exemption provisions of October, 1862, would be abrogated, and the general breakdown of law and order influenced many men to resume their hiding while many others escaped into Union areas. Heatwole describes the exodus as being so complete that "the Sunday congregations were composed of only a few old men, little boys, and the women. . . ." He describes the meetings as "made all the more solemn because the women nearly always wept during the time the sermon was preached." [33]

During these strenuous months in 1864 several articles appeared in the *Register* which tended to bring the Mennonites and Dunkers into public attention in an unfavorable light. On February 28, 1864, an article admonished them to "go to work . . . and raise all the provisions which their farms could possibly produce. . . . We have heard it stated that some of them did not intend to raise more upon their farms than will be necessary to pay their taxes." The article insisted that if true, "the Confederate Congress . . . should . . ." change the law so "as to put them into the ranks of the army." [34]

Still more provocative was an article appearing on March 4, 1864, which stated:

> We have been informed that some of our German friends who have been exempted from military duty, have declared their intention to raise no more bread and meat than . . . necessary for their own use. The Secretary of War has already been appraised of these facts, and will . . . be furnished with the names of the parties making such unpatriotic statements. If we can ascertain who they are . . . we will not only publish their names to the world, but will ourselves draw up a petition to the Congress. . . . Men who will not serve the great cause . . . ought to be put in the front ranks of our armies and if possible made food for gun powder. [35]

One week later a more positive article appeared which shows evidence of response to the former articles on the part of Mennonite and Dunker leaders.

> We have been assured by several of the leading members of the churches of Tunkers and Mennonites in this county that they will to the extent of their

ability do their duty to the country in this crisis. They will . . . raise all they can and will not tolerate indolence . . . in the members . . . able to work. They inform us that a member who shall be guilty of the sin of refusing . . . shall be excommunicated . . . and thus be obliged to go into the army. Both branches of these churches . . . have resolved to "lay by" a portion for the poor outside of their respective communions. It has always been a part of their policy to take care of their own poor: but now they go a step beyond this . . . this is the . . . spirit of an intelligent, enlightened Christianity. . . . [36]

Another article, published on March 18, held these people to be ideal loyal citizens who "feed more soldiers and horses than any other people of the boasting kind." They " . . . never turn away any that are in want, where they have it possibly to spare . . . and . . . the refugees . . . who have been driven from their homes by the fiendish Yankee enemy, could hardly have remained amongst us if it had not been for the kindness of the Tunker and Mennonite friends. . . ." [37]

On August 12, 1864, several unidentified persons contributed an article which inferred that some Dunkers and Mennonites were making "terrible exactions" of "poor people, especially of our soldiers' families for the necessaries of life." Again the threat of removing the exemption clause is made. [38]

These articles illustrate the varied and rather fluctuating sentiment held concerning the Mennonites and Dunkers and served to keep them and their peculiar stand in the public eye. Undoubtedly they would have preferred less publicity.

Chapter 8

DESTRUCTION AND FAMINE

During 1864 the Shenandoah Valley again played a significant role in the war as it did in 1862 when "Stonewall Jackson carried out a series of maneuvers aimed at keeping the Federals from moving troops from Western Virginia to join McClellan in his Peninsular campaign. Jackson succeeded spectacularly, but his accidental death at Chancellorsville in early May, 1863, forced the Confederates to choose another leader for the 1864 Valley campaign.

The activities of the Federal troops in the Valley in the spring of 1864 obligated General Lee to detach sizable units from his much-needed defense forces around Richmond which was beset by the Union forces under Grant. At this time Union Major General Franz-Sigel pushed up the Valley and on May 14 fought a losing engagement at New Market and was replaced by Major General David Hunter who promptly recovered New Market and pushed toward Harrisonburg. While at New Market, Hunter sent out foragers for sheep, grain, and flour. [1]   Moving south through Harrisonburg on June 2, apparently foragers continued to collect supplies. Peter Blosser made claims for property taken in June, 1864, by Hunter's army. [2]   Hunter clashed with Confederate Brigadier General John D. Imboden at Piedmont forcing the Confederates to abandon Staunton and retreat toward Lynchburg to which point Lee had sent Lieutenant General Jubal A. Early to begin a campaign to clear the Valley of Hunter and to threaten Washington. After stopping Hunter at Lynchburg, Early pursued him, at which time Hunter sidetracked into West Virginia freeing the Valley for Early's advance. Early hastily pushed down the Valley and amazed the Union capital by appearing in its suburbs on July 11, which unknown to Early, was scarcely defended until the arrival of Union reinforcements. The next night Early escaped with his army and returned to the Valley.

Chagrined at Early's escape from Washington, Grant determined to crush him, insisting in a communication to Major General Halleck on July 14 that if Early gets out of Maryland "he should have upon his heels veterans, militiamen, men on horseback, everything that can be got to follow to eat out Virginia clear and clean as far as they go, so that the crows flying over it for the balance of this season will have to carry their provender with them." [3]   In another communication to Halleck the next day Grant stated: "If Hunter cannot get to Gordonsville and Charlottesville to cut the railroad, he should make all the Valley south of the B and O road a desert as high as possible. I do not mean that houses should be burned, but all provisions and stock should be removed, and the people notified to move out.[4]

Early dislodged the Federal forces at Kernstown and sent Brigadier General John McCauseland to burn Chambersburg in retaliation for Federal destruction in the Valley if that town refused an indemnity payment. Grant, sensing that Early's success in retention of the Valley would present a menace to the Union, determined to send against him an overwhelming force. Early would have to be either crushed or else driven back so as to relieve the Union campaign against Richmond of a constant hindrance.

On August 5 Grant repeated his instructions to General Hunter to devastate the Valley in the following words:

> In pushing up the Shenandoah Valley . . . it is desirable that nothing should be left to invite the enemy to return. Take all provisions, forage and stock wanted for the use of your command; such as cannot be consumed, destroy. It is not desirable that the buildings should be destroyed; they should rather be protected; but the people should be informed that so long as an army can subsist among them recurrences of these raids must be expected, and we are determined to stop them at all hazards. Bear in mind the object is to drive the enemy south, and to do this you want to keep him always in sight. Be guided in your course by the course he takes. Make your own arrangements for supplies of all

kinds, giving regular vouchers for such as may be taken from loyal citizens in the country through which you march. 5

The agricultural resources of the Valley were more essential than ever in 1864 and without them the army of Northern Virginia would starve. Control of the Valley became a grim necessity at least until the summer's crops were harvested, even at the expense of weakening Lee's army still more, which was now desperately holding on at Petersburg.

General Hunter was eventually relieved of his command of the Valley forces and General Philip H. Sheridan, a cavalry officer, was placed in temporary command of a newly constituted Middle Military District on August 7, 1864. On September 21 he was given permanent command. Grant furnished Sheridan a top-notch cavalry to enable him to carry out the destruction in the Valley.

Although Sheridan had about twice the number of men as Early, he had to contend with the guerrilla forces of Colonel John S. Mosby who operated independent of the regular Confederate forces in northwest Virginia. The deceptive tactics of these bushwhackers bred sheer hatred in the minds of Union men and were distasteful to many Confederates and in time became unpopular because of the retributions made by enraged Federal commanders. Yet Mosby and his men were worth many divisions to the Confederacy because their effective raids required many more Union troops to protect communications and supply lines.

In a major battle at Winchester on September 19, Sheridan won a decisive victory which along with General William Sherman's victory at Atlanta, Georgia, gave the North much-needed encouragement. On September 22, at Fishers Hill, Sheridan forced the Confederates to stampede up the Valley opening the way to Harrisonburg into which town Sheridan marched on September 25. From Harrisonburg Sheridan dispatched cavalry forces into the areas to the South. Major General Alfred T. Torbert was sent through Staunton to Waynesboro to blow up the railroad tunnel at Rockfish Gap; Torbert then returned, burning mills, forage, and foodstuffs and taking as many cattle as possible. Major General Wesley Merritt was sent on a swing through Piedmont and Staunton on a similar mission. The effect of these Union movements was to make the most productive region of the Valley desolate and useless to Early and the Confederates.

The destruction already accomplished by Union forces by this time is depicted by a Confederate private as follows:

> Our army was now reduced to only 5000 or 6000 men and seemed badly discouraged and looked like they thought it was useless to fight any longer. We had an elevated position and could see Yankees out in the valley driving off the horses, cattle, sheep and killing the hogs and burning all the barns and shocks of corn and wheat in the fields

and destroying everything that could feed or shelter man or beast. They burnt nearly all the dwelling houses, the valley was soon filled with smoke. [6]

On October 3, Lieutenant John R. Meigs, Sheridan's chief engineer, on whose intimate familiarity with the Valley Sheridan relied heavily, was fatally shot within Union lines just out side of Dayton. Concluding that the killers of Meigs lived in the vicinity, Sheridan decided that a drastic warning to the people was called for. Brigadier General George A. Custer was directed to burn all houses within a radius of five miles. [7]

Margaret H. Rhodes tells of soldiers coming to her house and allowing her fifteen minutes to get out at the time when Lieutenant Meigs was killed. Her house was not burned, however. [8] After Custer began his task, Sheridan upon reflecting withdrew the order after a few houses were burned, ordering Custer to confine his efforts to gathering all able-bodied men as prisoners. [9] Wayland states that about twenty places in the neighborhood were burned. [10] Noah Wenger, who lived near the spot where Meigs was killed, left with his family after which his barn was burned but not his house. [11] Benjamin Wenger's house, barn, and outbuildings were burned and all of his livestock, grain, and growing timber was lost. [12] Abraham Blosser's house and barn were also destroyed. [13]

L. J. Heatwole, who witnessed the destruction, described the burning, stating that:

. . . between the hour of 3 p.m. and nightfall the torch had been applied to all the mills, barns and numbers of dwellings from Dayton westward to Coakleytown and northward as far as Dale Enterprise.

Nearly all families of this section spent the night . . . out in the open with great fires raging upon every side and what little sleep that was had was taken on sleeping couches stretched on the sod. The early morning hours . . . were marked by a dense blanket of smoke and fog that had settled over the country as it were to hide from view the awful effect of the great holocaust of fire of the evening before. [14]

Michael Shank after arriving in Pennsylvania described the situation at this time as follows:

When General Sheridan's army came into the Valley of Virginia, the "Boys," or prowlers, contrary to the General's orders, commenced pilfering, robbing and plundering, squads of them would go to citizens houses in almost frantic appearance, their faces speaking terror to the inhabitants, while they were searching every room from cellar to garret, breaking open bureau drawers, chests and closets taking whatever suited their fancy, such as money, watches, jewelry, wearing apparel, etc., at the same time threatening to shoot the inmates of the house if they followed after them. In the meantime our horses, cows and cattle were taken, the grain house was broken open and robbed of its contents and when the body of the army passed up thousands upon thousands passed over my farm in a number of columns through corn and cornfields; thus they continued their work of destruction until they reached Staunton or its vicinity, from whence they commenced retreating and burning barns, mills, etc. For several days before we left we saw great columns of smoke rising like dark clouds almost from one mountain to the other. 15

The anxiety and fear which Mennonites felt in these days are described by D. H. Landis in a letter written to the *Herald of Truth* one month later after he had reached Ohio.

> We were for the last four years living in a some- what disturbed and uneasy state of mind . . . in con- sequence of the national calamity that is now exist- ing. We were not subjected to as much suffering in this space of time, as some in other parts of the Southern States, until the latter part of September, when the calamity grew severer and we sought to flee where more peace of mind could be enjoyed, and where we would be remote from the noise of war; for here we could not enjoy the privilege of assembling ourselves together to worship the true and living God as we often wished. Some of our churches were destroyed so that we could not convene on such occasions. . . .
>
> We held our conference on the last Friday and Saturday in August in Weaver's Church, and on Sunday we observed the communion of the Lord's Supper. We had quite a large meeting. The house was principally filled with members who nearly all partook of the sacrament. 16

The destruction carried out by Sheridan during his stay in the vicinity of Harrisonburg, in addition to the deprivations experienced earlier, prompted many finally to leave the Valley until after the war. General Sheridan,

aware of the attitude of Confederate sympathizers toward the religious objectors and those who sympathized
with the Union, offered to "furnish one team and wagon
to each Union sympathizer to transport his belongings
and family beyond the boundaries of the Confederacy."
On the very day that Meigs "was killed a number of
persons, whose property was burned, had already loaded what they could take on one wagon and had moved
as far as Harrisonburg."[17]   That many of the religious
objectors availed themselves of this opportunity for protected departure from the war-devastated Valley is
proved by the notation by General Sheridan that from
"the vicinity of Harrisonburg over four hundred wagon-
loads of refugees have been sent back to Martinsburg.
Most of these people were Dunkers. . . . "[18]   L. J.
Heatwole claimed that a number of Mennonite families
and most of the sixteen- and seventeen-year-old boys
left at this time.[19]

Heatwole in another source relates how Sheridan's
soldiers made daily raids during this time "over much
of the farm section of the county, where bread, bacon,
butter, lard, and poultry were either carried away in
person by the soldiers or transferred to camp in
forage wagons that followed the main roads in great
number." Fattened hogs and beef cattle were slaughtered on the spot, and horses, cows, calves, and sheep
driven away in large droves.[20]

One Mennonite stated how he came to a decision
to leave the area as follows:

The Union army came up the Valley sweeping everything before them like a wild hurricane; there was nothing left for man or beast; neither was there anything needed for beasts, as they left no beast from the horse down to the chicken; all was taken. So we felt as though we could not subsist; and besides, they were burning down barns and mills in every direction around us. Not feeling willing to stay and and again have the rebel army over us, searching for something to eat, I went to Harrisonburg Head Quarters to see about getting away.21

Another Mennonite relates how that as the Federal army carried out its destruction

. . . we chose rather to leave all behind to go to a land of peace and quietness than to endure the terrors about to be inflicted upon us as well as that . . . which was yet awaiting us. I immediately went to camp and applied for two teams which were soon . . . to my house and about 3 o'clock . . . we commenced packing our clothing, wearing apparel, . . . and a few other articles, leaving . . . nearly all of our household and kitchen furniture. We did not get off until sometime after dark. The rain was falling fast at the time, which made the circumstance . . . still more unpleasant. . . .

Thus we started, some of the children were crying to go to bed, and some for bread, neither of which could be granted under the circumstances. . . . We hastened . . . until we reached Harrisonburg . . . and the train not being ready to leave, we remained there from Monday night until Wednesday. During that time I went back home to see the state of things there, and found the destruction completed, the dwelling house and barn with all their contents and all the out buildings were entirely consumed by the flames. [22]

Numerous Mennonite families secured passes and transportation northward. [23] In addition there were a number of young men at or near military age who traveled along also. Hartman states that there were six boys he knew very well with whom he joined to arrange to go north with Sheridan. They were ushered into General Sheridan's presence and given passes by him personally and were allowed to find any of their horses for their own use. Hartman came back home for a saddle and returned to the camp in readiness to leave with the wagon train the next day. Not all who hoped to get to go along north with Sheridan succeeded in doing so. [24]

L. J. Heatwole describes this day on which Sheridan started to move north as follows:

By the hour of 9 a.m., Federal troops were everywhere in motion driving livestock northward and applying the torch to barns and mills that remained from the day before. At a later hour the boom of cannon, the bursting of shells, and the rattle of musketry were heard, still later soldiers appeared in the line along the tops of higher hills, minnie balls whistled sharply overhead and cavalry men were seen galloping at top speed northward along the roads and over the fields . . . leaving in their path a sum of destruction that baffles the pen to describe. [25]

It was on October 6 that Sheridan started to move the long wagon train northward led by the infantry

Dunkers and Mennonites Getting Passes to Go North

This sketch by J. E. Taylor shows Commissary W. H. Douglas giving information and instructions to refugees who are in the process of leaving with General Sheridan's supply train as it moves north out of the burned-out, wasted Shenandoah Valley. (Photo secured from Western Reserve Historical Society, Cleveland, Ohio, and by courtesy of Grant Stoltzfus.)

and artillery and covered in the rear by Torbert's cavalry. Hartman describes the train as being sixteen miles long and comprised of 1,600 wagons. [26] The cavalry stretched across the Valley from the Blue Ridge to the North Mountain burning mills, barns, and crops. Sheridan describes the destruction carried out in an October 7 dispatch to Grant from Woodstock as follows:

I commenced moving back from Port Republic, Mount Crawford, and Harrisonburg yesterday morning. The grain and forage in advance of these points had previously been destroyed. In moving back to this point the whole country, from the Blue Ridge to the North Mountain, has been made entirely untenable for a rebel army. I have destroyed over 2000 barns filled with wheat, hay and farming implements; over 70 mills filled with flour and wheat; have driven in front of the army over four herd of stock and have killed and issued to the troops not less than 3000 sheep. . . . A large number of horses have been obtained. [27]

The army moved slowly down the Valley as it carried out its work of destruction. Reaching New Market after dark in pouring rain the refugees must surely have been uncomfortable and discouraged. On October 7 they reached Woodstock at dusk. Bridges burned by the Confederate guerrillas hindered their progress at a few points and when General Early learned of the Union trek down the Valley he followed cautiously. [28] Early's cavalry provoked minor incidents with Sheridan's cavalry units which prompted the Union general to order his cavalry to pursue the annoying Confederates at Tom's Brook on October 9 causing the latter to flee wildly in retreat. [29]

Meanwhile the refugees continued northward reaching Newtown on October 8, Winchester on the ninth, and Martinsburg on the eleventh. Hartman states that a "number of our own people . . . would get together in the evening and sing." This, he claims, the soldiers enjoyed very much. [30]

General Sheridan had agreed to furnish transportation to Martinsburg only. Here some of the refugees secured boxes to pack their goods to place on the train westward.[31] Peter Hartman rode to Hagerstown on his horse while others went to the same destination on hired hacks.[32]

Meanwhile the desolation in the Valley was so desperate that the strength of the Confederate forces was soon seriously affected. Soldiers from the Valley whose families were in want had ample excuse to desert the Confederate service. In an appeal for exemption from conscription for those from the area, the presiding justice of Rockingham County wrote as follows:

> Many who are liable are without a pound of meat, bread, or anything to live on, to say nothing of firewood. It will require the daily and hourly exertions of the poor and those who have been burnt out to secure a scanty subsistence to sustain life during the winter. When the soldier now in the army learns that his neighbor, on whom his family have leaned for support during all this war, is himself called into service and his family . . . are sure to suffer, he will become uneasy in his place and will weigh the duty he owes to his family; and what the promptings of nature would be is not difficult to determine. . . . We have no slave labor and this call taxes our principal working force. What is to become of our corn crop? What is to become of any spring crop?[33]

The winter of 1864-65 was a very difficult one for the Valley now that virtually all supplies were taken and much property destroyed. By building temporary

shelter and by sharing the scanty supplies which remained, they eked out a meager existence. Their
plight prompted them to have things in common. [34]

The losses caused by the raids of the Union army
were undoubtedly very extensive. An estimate made by
an officially appointed committee consisting of local
officials and prominent citizens, however, was apparently exaggerated. After surveying the destruction and loss
in all parts of the county, this committee estimated the
total loss as twenty-five million, five hundred thousand
dollars. [35]   Wayland holds that the loss was actually
much less in value in terms of the property values
then existing. He estimates the loss to be somewhat in
excess of two million dollars. [36]   Wayland's reasoning
seems to be substantiated by the value of claims made
by professed Unionists. A total a three hundred and
eleven claims made by residents of the county added up
to two hundred and seventy-five thousand, eight hundred dollars. [37]

Chapter *9*

SUMMARY AND CONCLUSIONS

This then is the record of events and experiences associated with the attempts of Mennonites in the Confederacy to give expression to their basic pacifist beliefs. It is not a faultless record to be sure. But the sincerity of these simple agrarian people can hardly be disputed.

The Civil War was a period of real danger to the civil liberties of the individual American. The suspension of the writ of habeas corpus, the tendency to allow the executive to assume extraordinary powers, and the very military nature of the war itself tended to bend the individual to the will of the state. In the South the more desperate situation and the consequent need for all available troops tended to place more pressure on the objector to war. At the same time the Southern people generally admired military titles, and military educational institutions enjoyed a prominence all their own. [1] These factors help to explain the more difficult lot of the religious objector in the South as compared to the North.

The stand of the Virginia Mennonites during the Civil War is a fine record. One must keep in mind that they comprised a very small group. Flights to the North gradually dwindled their total still more. Their determination to practice their faith at the time when it was most difficult speaks for the spiritual quality of the group generally. Most of the young men stood the test of government coercion. If they compromised by going into the military in 1861, as many of them did, they at least refused to cooperate in killing "the enemy." One must bear in mind that there was no alternative to joining the military other than becoming a deserter. Those who joined but refused to shoot were able to bring the issue to the minds of their fellow soldiers and to their military superiors. At the same time the activities of the church leaders brought the issue to the attention of the highest civilian officials.

The vigorous leadership of Bishop Samuel Coffman is one of the most heartening parts of the whole account. His courage in a very difficult time enhances his stature as a leader in the crisis.

It is appropriate, however, to probe into the ethical implications of hiring substitutes to take one's place in the military. This practice was quite common among Mennonites as well as among Dunkers, although Mennonites in the South were hardly less consistent here than their brethren in the North. [2]   To be the means of another person entering military service for one's own exemption is hardly compatible with a peace witness. The rather ready willingness to accept activities not directly involved with battle in such services as teamsters, cooks, and other activities might be questioned also, for to be in any part of the military organization is to enhance its success in its sole purpose, that is, to defeat the enemy.

A most important consideration is the "definite pro-Union sentiment" which was shown by the Mennonites in the Confederacy. Their constant contacts with the larger Mennonite groups in the North, the fears which the secession of the South generated, the lack of States' Rights sentiment and sectional feeling among them all point in the direction of a pro-North stance on the part of these people. Most of all they could not condone a rebellion against an established government ordained by God. Typical was the case of Samuel Shank, a Mennonite and minister who regarded the United States government as his government and considered the Confederate government a rebel government. [3] The renowned local historian, John Wayland, includes the Mennonites among those who "remained loyal to the Union." [4] It was this pro-Union sentiment which caused friction in their communities, increasingly so as the Confederate situation became more desperate. John F. Lewis recognized the consistently pro-Union stance of the Mennonites when he testified before the Joint Committee on Reconstruction in February, 1866, stating:

There are a great many men . . . who now profess to have been Union men all the time, but who were not known as such during the war. Of these I did not speak; I spoke of those who were known as uncompromising Union men throughout. There were very few such persons in the State. The Dunkard population . . . were generally loyal and are still loyal; but they are a timid set of men, who take very little part in politics; and their influence is pretty much lost to the State. Leave that element out of the question, and the Union men are in a very meagre minority. [5]

It is true that statements were made by certain military officials characterizing the Mennonites and Dunkers as loyal to the Confederacy.[6] Such statements appear rather superficial, however, when considered in light of the many more statements and attitudes indicating a pro-Union stand. Even after the war Mennonites were maligned at times for their stand during the war. [7]

However, Mennonites in this time hardly imbibed the intense nationalistic fervor which enabled the Union to pursue her goal of the defeat of the Confederacy. The essential basis of their opposition was not political but religious. The Claims Commission sensed this clearly and expressed it in connection with their refusal to grant the claim of Gabriel D. Heatwole, explaining their action as follows:

We do not think him justified upon his own statement. He was obviously opposed to war upon religious principle. . . . It is rather to be inferred from his general conduct that he was opposed to the rebellion, but he acted rather according to the rules of his church to keep out of the war than from strong Union principle. 8

The writer cannot conclude this study without giving special recognition to the Dunkers of that period for their courageous leadership in speaking their convictions which were virtually identical with those of the Mennonites, so much so that any concessions made to Dunkers were in effect concessions to the Mennonites as well. There was a certain degree of cooperation in presenting petitions for the securing of exemptions, in processing the release of prisoners, and in the operation of the escape system for deserters and refugees. These two groups had every reason for cooperating and both have suffered from the failure to foster the further development of these attempts at cooperation of the wartime years. The postwar decades saw both groups again going their separate ways tending to accentuate their minor differences and avoiding their striking similarities.

FOOTNOTES

Chapter 1

1 Edward Needles Wright, *Conscientious Objectors in the Civil War*, Perpetua Edition (A. S. Barnes and Company, 1961), p. 20.

2. Letter of Nov. 5, 1928, from L. J. Heatwole to Edward Needles Wright in Historical Library and Archives, Eastern Mennonite College, Harrisonburg, Va.

3. D. H. Zigler, *History of the Brethren in Virginia* (Elgin, Ill.: Brethren Publishing House, 1914), Chaps. V and VI; Wright, *op. cit.*, Chaps. I and III. These sources elaborate on the Dunkers and Quakers respectively. Mennonites are treated in this paper.

4. *Minutes of the Virginia Mennonite Conference*, Action 14 (Historical Library and Archives, Eastern Mennonite College, Harrisonburg, Va.), p. 6.

5. *Rockingham Register* [Harrisonburg, Va.], March 25, 1864.

6. *The Confession of Faith of the Christians Known by the Name of Mennonites with Nine Reflections by Peter Burkholder*. Translated from the German by Joseph Funk (Winchester, Va., 1837), Article Twenty-Seventh, pp. 218 f. Historical Library and Archives, Eastern Mennonite College. This was the P. J. Twisck Confession as found in the *Martyrs Mirror*, and the name Burkholder attached to the document is misleading, for it was Joseph Funk who most likely wrote the Introduction and translated and compiled the volume. Harold S. Bender, "Peter Burkholder," *Mennonite Encyclopedia*, Vol. I, pp. 477 f.

7. *Ibid.*, p. 219.

8. *Ibid.*, pp. 219-25.

9. John G. Nicolay and John Hay, *Abraham Lincoln, A History* (New York: The Century Company, 1890), Vol. VI, pp. 327-29.

10. Fernando Cartland, *Southern Heroes or the Friends in Wartime* (Cambridge: The Riverside Press, 1895), p. 127. See Wright, *op. cit.*, p. 121.

11. J. B. Jones, *A Rebel War Clerk's Diary* (Philadelphia: J. B. Lippincott and Company, 1866), Vol. II, pp. 428 and 442. See Wright, *op. cit.*, p. 139.

12. Clifford Dowdey, *The Land They Fought For: The Story of the South as the Confederacy*, 1832-1865 (Garden City, New York: Doubleday and Company, 1955), pp. 169 f.

13. James G. Randall and David Donald, *The Civil War and Reconstruction* (Boston: D. C. Heath and Company, 1961), p. 514.

14. Ella Lonn, *Desertion During the Civil War* (New York and London: The Century Company, 1908), pp. 118 f.

Chapter 2

1. *Register*, Nov. 9, 1860, and Nov. 16, 1860.

2. Ralph A. Wooster, *The Secession Conventions of the South* (Princeton: Princeton University Press, 1962), p. 147.

3. Benjamin Funk (ed), *Life of John Kline, Collated from His Diary* (Elgin, Ill.: Brethren Publishing House, 1900), p. 439.

4. Zigler, *op. cit.*, pp. 95 f.

5. E. Merton Coulter, *The Confederate States of America 1861-1865* (Vol. VII

of *A History of the South* by Wendell Holmes Stephenson and E. Merton Coulter, eds. 10 vols.; Baton Rouge, La.: Louisiana State University Press, 1950), p. 41.

6. Allan Nevins, *The War for Union*, Vol. I, *The Impoverished War, 1861-1862* (Vol. V of *The Ordeal of the Union*, 5 vols. to date; New York: Charles Scribner's Sons, 1959), p. 103.

7. *Register*, May 17, 1861.

8. *Ibid.*

9. Funk, *op. cit.*, p. 440.

10. See page 48.

11. *Register*, Feb. 15, 1861.

12. See page 8.

13. From the testimony of these persons in their separate claims made to the Civil War Claims Commission. National Archives. Record Group No. 56. Claim No. 9739—Samuel Shank; Claim No. 9519—Samuel Coffman; Claim No. 21843 —Daniel J. Good; Claim No. 16500—Peter Blosser; Claim No. 9123—David Breneman.

14. Claim No. 8701—John Geil. From *Digest of Disallowed Claims: Summary Reports of the Commissioners of Claims in all Cases Reported to Congress as Disallowed under the Act of March 3, 1871*, p. 389. Old House of Representatives Office Building, House File Room, *1873 Report*.

15. Claims Commission, Claim No. 15912—Jacob Wenger; also Claim No. 21844 —Jacob Geil.

16. *Ibid.*, Claim No. 21844—Jacob Geil.

17. *Ibid.*, Claim No. 21856—John Brunk; Claim No. 9521—Daniel P. Good; Claim No. 8997—Abraham Heatwole; Claim No. 21831—Gabriel D. Heatwole; Claim No. 16949—David E. Rhodes testifies in claim of Estate of John Rhodes; Claim No. 21837—Frederick S. Rhodes; Claim No. 21836—Henry L. Rhodes; Claim No. 9781—Jacob Shank, Jr.; *Digest of Disallowed Claims*, House File Room, Claim No. 8336—Emanuel Suter; Claim No. 15531—Noah Wenger— *1874 Report*.

18. *Ibid.*, Claim No. 21836—Henry L. Rhodes.

Chapter 3

1. Harry A. Brunk, *History of the Mennonites in Virginia: 1727-1900*, Vol. I (Harrisonburg, Va.: Published by the author, 1959), p. 157.

2. Letter to Governor John Letcher, Executive Papers, Virginia State Library.

3. Harry A. Brunk, *Life of Peter S. Hartman Including His Lecture: Reminiscences of the Civil War and Articles by the Hartman Family* (Published by the Hartman Family, 1937), p. 49. According to Barbara Coffman, who claims the basis of fact for the events she describes even though she does not substantiate them, two uniformed men entered the church while Bishop Samuel Coffman was preaching. One of them is described as an officer who "marched to the front of the room where he seated himself and listened to the remainder of the sermon." Although surprised, Coffman did not become excited but continued preaching. When calling for a hymn after his sermon, the officer arose and briefly but emphatically gave notice that all young men between eighteen and forty-five were to report for military training. After the officer left, Coffman rose and

spoke to his congregation in choking and trembling voice. Barbara Coffman, *His Name Was John: The Life Story of an Early Mennonite Leader* (Scottdale, Pa.: Herald Press, 1964), p. 26.

4. L. J. Heatwole, "A Brief History of the Mennonite Congregations in Virginia and West Virginia," Historical Library and Archives, Eastern Mennonite College, p. 5.

5. Claims Commission, Claim No. 9527—Margaret H. Rhodes.

6. Charles D. Breneman, *A History of the Descendants of Abraham Breneman* (Elida, Ohio: Published by the author, 1939), p. 39.

7. Compiled Service Records of Confederate Soldiers Who Served in Virginia. On microfilm in National Archives.

8. This record states that he refused to go into military service until threatened to be taken by force. He was in the service from six to eight months after he escaped leaving his team on the road. A substitute was eventually sent in his place until the 1862 exemption law was passed. National Archives, Claim No. 21856—John Brunk. See also Joseph H. Wenger, *History of the Descendants of J. Conrad Geil and His Son Jacob Geil* (Elgin, Ill., 1914), p. 90.

9. Geil furnished a substitute. When his substitute's time expired, Geil escaped with the seventy-four who were apprehended and imprisoned at Richmond. See pages 47-56

10. See pages 32-33

11. Refused to go into militia and hid with Daniel J. Good in neighborhood. Accompanied the seventy-four who fled and were apprehended and imprisoned at Richmond. Claims Commission, Claim No. 21831—Gabriel Heatwole.

12. See page 74.

13. See page 33.

14. See pages 33, 37, and 43.

15. Fled with group of seventy-four who were apprehended and imprisoned at Richmond. See pages 47-56.

16. *Ibid.*

17. *Ibid.*

18. *Ibid.*

19. *Ibid.*

20. See page 38. Worked on nitre production.

21. Company E of the First Regiment of the Virginia Militia, for example, collected at Lacey Spring on July 6, 1861. *Hardesty's Historical and Geographical Encyclopedia* (Richmond: H. H. Hardesty and Company, Publishers, 1884), p. 401.

22. Charles E. Nair, *John Kline.* (Unpublished manuscript in possession of Agnes Kline, 1952.) See also Heatwole, *op. cit.*, p. 6.

23 Heatwole, *op. cit.*, p. 6. See also chapter by Heatwole in J. S. Hartzler and Daniel Kauffman, *Mennonite Church History* (Scottdale, Pa.; Mennonite Book and Tract Society, 1905), Chap. XIII.

24. Nair, *op. cit.*, p. 176.

25. Heatwole, *op. cit.*, p. 6. Hartzler and Kauffman, *op. cit.*, p. 208.

26. Brunk, *Life of P. S. Hartman*, p. 49.

27. Edith Wenger Morgan, "Stories My Father Told Us" (Unpublished, nd). Booklet in possession of Mrs. Earl Grove, daughter of L. J. Heatwole.

28. Claims Commission, Claim No. 15912—Jacob Wenger.

29. Brunk, *Life of P. S. Hartman*, pp. 49, 50.

30. *War of the Rebellion, Official Records,* Series I, Vol. XII, Part III, p. 835.

31. Special Order to Lieutenant Colonel J. R. Jones of 33rd Volunteer Regiment of Virginia Milita from Major General Jackson. Historical Library and Archives, Eastern Mennonite College.

32. *Register,* Aug. 2, 1861.

33. *Official Records,* pp. 841 f.

34. *Register,* July 5, 1861.

35. S. F. Sanger and D. Hays, *The Olive Branch of Peace and Goodwill to Men* (Elgin, Ill.: Brethren Publishing House, 1907), p. 54.

36. *Register,* Aug. 9, 1861.

37. *Ibid.,* Sept. 13, 1861.

38. Heatwole claimed that most of the Mennonite men went home after four months. *Op. cit.,* p. 6.

39. *Ibid.*

40. Claims Commission, Claim No. 9527—Margaret Rhodes.

41. Heatwole, Letter of Nov. 5, 1928, to Edward Needles Wright. Hartman states as follows: Just about the time the war began, the Mennonite Church decided that if any of the members would voluntarily go to war, they would voluntarily go out of the church, without a church trial or anything of the kind. It was a dangerous thing to have a church trial. The church was very loyal and stuck together well. Only two brothers, Shenk by name, voluntarily went into the war. One of them was wounded and taken prisoner and died in prison. The other one came home but never came back into the church. Brunk, *Life of P. S. Hartman.*

42. Adjutant Inspector General's Office, Letters Received. No. 1313, National Archives. Record Group No. 94. The apparent Mennonite names are Henry Heatwole, Shem Heatwole, David M. Weaver, and Jacob Heatwole.

43. See page 30.

44. *Digest of Disallowed Claims,* 1874 Report, p. 580. Claim No. 8701—Joseph E. Niswander.

45. Claims Commission, Claim No. 21836—Henry L. Rhodes.

46. Bell Irvin Wiley, *The Common Soldier in the Civil War: Book II, The Life of Johnny Reb* (New York: Grosset and Dunlap, 1943), pp. 125 f. Zigler claimed that Dunkers paid from eight hundred to fifteen hundred dollars each. Zigler, *op. cit.,* p. 98.

47. Coulter, *op. cit.,* p. 319.

48. Claims Commission, Claim No. 16509—Peter Blosser.

49. Claims Commission, Claim No. 21844—Jacob Geil.

50. Daniel K. Cassel, *History of the Mennonites.* See A Historical Sketch of the Early Mennonites in Virginia, communicated by Abraham Blosser, editor of the *Watchful Pilgrim* (Philadelphia: Published by the author, 1888), pp. 136 f.

51. Claims Commission, Claim No. 9125—George Brunk. The records of this claim are under Congressional Jurisdiction, Record Group No. 123. Brunk's claim was taken to the Court of Claims by his attorney, but here too, as before the Claims Commission, his claim was not held valid.

52. See page 91.

53. Claims Commission, Claim No. 21836—Henry L. Rhodes.
54. Claims Commission, Claim No. 21856—John Brunk.
55. Claims Commission, Claim No. 9123, David Breneman. *Digest of Disallowed Claims, 1873 Report*, Claim No. 16921—Henry Geil; Claim No. 8701—John Geil; Claim No. 9781—Jacob Shank, Jr.; Claim No. 9739—Samuel Shank; Claim No. 9778—Isaac Wenger.

Chapter 4

1. Claims Commission, Claim No. 21856—John Brunk.
2. Abraham Blosser hid himself in a secluded hollow in' the mountains about sixteen miles from his home rather than escape North so that he could keep in contact with his family. Cassel, *op. cit.*, p. 136. Gabriel D. Heatwole and Daniel J. Good hid together in their own neighborhood. Claims Commission, Claim No. 71856—Daniel J. Good.
3. Claims Commission, Claim No. 21856—John Brunk.
4. Claims Commission, Claim No. 21844—Jacob Geil.
5. Claims Commission, Claim No. 21843—Daniel J. Good.
6. Claims Commission, Claim No. 9521—Daniel P. Good.
7. Claims Commission, Claim No. 21836—Henry L. Rhodes.
8. Claims Commission, Claim No. 16949—Estate of John Rhodes,
9. Claims Commission, Claim No. 9527—Margaret Rhodes.
10. Claims Commission, Claim No. 15912—Jacob Wenger.
11. Claims Commission, Claim No. 9521—Daniel P. Good.
12. Claims Commission, Claim No. 9739—Samuel Shank; Claim No. 8941—Joseph Beery, Claim No. 9519—Samuel Coffman; Claim No. 9125—George Brunk.
13. Claims Commission, Claim No. 21843—Daniel J. Good.
14. Claims Commission, Claim No. 16949—Estate of John Rhodes.
15. Claims Commission, Claim No. 21844—Jacob Geil.
16. Sanger and Hays,: *op. cit.*, pp. 76, 77.
17. Claims Commission, Claim No. 21856—John Brunk.
18. Claims Commission, Claim No. 21843—Daniel J. Good.
19. Claims Commission, Claim No. 9527—Margaret Rhodes.
20. Claims Commission, Claim No. 21836—Henry L. Rhodes.
21. Claims Commission, Claim No. 16949—Estate of John Rhodes.
22. Claims Commission, Claim No. 21844—Jacob Geil.

Chapter 5

1. Dowdey, *op. cit.*, p. 174.
2. Harry A. Brunk, "Samuel Coffman," *The Mennonite Encyclopedia*, I (Scottdale, Pa.: Mennonite Publishing House, 1955), p. 634. See also Barbara Coffman, *op. cit.*, p. 25.
3. Sanger and Hays, *op. cit.*, pp. 60, 61.
4. Zigler, *op. cit.*, p. 174.
5. Brunk, *History*, *op. cit.*, pp. 360, 361.
6. Sanger and Hays, *op. cit.*, p. 61.
7. The "fine law" refers to the March, 1862, Virginia exemption provision,

See page 68. Claims Commission, Claim No. 21836—Henry L. Rhodes.

8. Zigler, *op. cit.*, pp. 103, 104.

9. John S. Funk in testimony on his father Jonathan Funk's claim tells of a group of eighteen in which his father was included. Claims Commission, Claim No. 2506—Jonathan Funk.

10. Sanger and Hays, *op. cit.*, pp. 76-78.

11. Sanger and Hays, *op. cit.*, p. 69. The first of these was Peter Blosser. Claims Commission, Claim No. 15572—Peter Blosser. The other escapee was David Miller, a Dunker. Sanger and Hays, *op. cit.*, pp. 80 f. The latter should not be confused with David M. Miller.

12. This includes two men not eligible for military service who accompanied the group. See footnote No. 32.

13. Brunk, *Life of P. S. Hartman*, p. 56.

14. Sanger and Hays, *op. cit.*, pp. 108 f.

15. *Ibid.*, p. 66. David M. Miller (not the escapee) stated in 1906 that the group started about March 13, 1862. Zigler, *op. cit.*, p. 104.

16. "We started from Samuel Berry's near Crissmans and went through Hopkins Gap. Then along over ridges across ravines and the Shenandoah mountain we arrived at Judy's on the South Fork where we stayed all night. The next day we crossed Ketterman's Mountain and came to the South Branch of the Potomac." Simeon Heatwole in Sanger and Hays, p. 109.

17. Joseph A. Miller describes the river as being fifty or more yards wide. *Ibid.*, p. 60.

18. David M. Miller, a Dunker member of the group, relates as follows: "When we got about a mile beyond Petersburg we saw some persons we thought were soldiers riding. They got ahead of us and stopped in a narrow place in the road. They took us back to Petersburg and searched us, but found no weapon except one small revolver, but some of us had Testaments." Zigler, *op. cit.*, p. 105. Joseph A. Miller, a brother of David and also a Dunker, relates that two men halted their journey just after going through Petersburg, "one in front and one in the rear. The man in front made use of some hard words, but the man in the rear was kind. We halted and at their solicitation we turned back to Petersburg." Sanger and Hays, *op. cit.*, p. 68.

19. *Ibid.*, pp. 68, 69 and 109. See also Claims Commission, Claim No. 15572—Peter Blosser. Also Brunk, *P. S. Hartman*, p. 56.

20. *Ibid.*, pp. 69, 80, 81.

21. *Ibid.*, p. 100.

22. Joseph A. Waddell, *Annals of Augusta County, Virginia, From 1726 to 1871* (Staunton, Va.: C. Russell Caldwell, Publisher, 1902), p. 466. This source describes the group as follows: "Some, if not all are simple-hearted, inoffensive people belonging to the Dunkard church, whose tenets forbid going to war. . . . There is something pitiful in the case of these people flying as they were to escape conscription and being taken like partridges on the mountains."

23. Sanger and Hays, *op. cit.*, pp. 70-72.

24. *Ibid.*, p. 110.

25. *Ibid.*, p. 71.

26. *Ibid.*, p. 71.

27. Simeon Heatwole, a member of the imprisoned group, referred to the prison as "Thunder Castle." *Ibid.*, p. 111. S. A. Sanger, whose brother David

and brother-in-law Benjamin Miller were part of the imprisoned group, claimed that the captives were placed in "Castle Thunder," an "old tobacco warehouse, with heavy brick walls, small windows, securely barred, and very unsanitary, as well as uninviting. . . ." *Ibid.*, p. 81. D. K. Cassel makes a similar claim, *op. cit.*, Cassel, p. 135. The writer of this thesis while working in the National Archives made his acquaintance with Robert Waitt, Jr., Secretary of the Civil War Centennial Committee for the city of Richmond. Mr. Waitt, an expert on Civil War maps of the city, informed me that the building described in the above account was surely not Libby Prison but Castle Thunder. He informed me that Libby Prison was only for officers.

28. Coulter, *op. cit.*, p. 89.

29. Sanger and Hays, *op. cit.*, p. 116.

30. *Ibid.*, p. 111.

31. Letters Received, Confederate Secretary of War, 444-B-1862, National Archives. Record Group 109.

32. *Official Records*, Series II, Vol. 3, p. 385, Report of S. S. Baxter.

33. Sanger and Hays, *op. cit.*, p. 71.

34. See Heatwole, *op. cit.*, p. 7. Also Brunk, *Life of P. S. Hartman*, p. 58.

35. Sanger and Hays, *op. cit.*, p. 72. Using the date which David M. Miller suggests as the time when the group started on their flight from the Valley, the calendar of events was likely as follows:

Thursday, March 13, 1862—Flight from Valley (See footnote No. 15.)

Saturday, March 15, 1862—Capture at Petersburg

Sunday, March 16, 1862—Arrival at Franklin

Monday, March 17, 1862—Arrival at Monterey

Wednesday, March 19, 1862—Arrival at Staunton (This conforms to Waddell's account.)

Thursday, March 20, 1862—Arrival in Richmond late at night

Friday, March 21, 1862—Moved into "Castle Thunder"

Assuming as Joseph A. Miller does that the group was kept at Richmond for thirty days and was absent from home for thirty-seven days, the calendar of later events was likely as follows:

Monday, April 14, 1862—Release from Castle Thunder

Saturday, April 19, 1862—Arrival at home

36. *Ibid.*, p. 107. Also Sanger and Hays, *op. cit.*, p. 61.

37. *Richmond Dispatch*, March 31, 1862.

38 Sanger and Hays, *op. cit.*, p. 63. J. M. Cline claimed that their stay here was for some days. Jackson Showalter (Zigler, *op. cit.*, p. 107), also in the group claimed the stay to be only one day. At Mount Jackson they first stayed in a large room. Later they were moved to the upper end of the town and placed in a small room under guard. At night they sometimes helped to load wagons.

39. This group was apparently already imprisoned in Harrisonburg when Elder John Kline was brought there. Funk, *op. cit.*, p. 448. J. M. Cline, one of the group, later claimed two weeks as the length of time of imprisonment at Harrisonburg. Sanger and Hays, *op. cit.*, p. 64. Joseph Beery also gives two weeks as the length of time. Claims Commission, Claim No. 8941—Joseph Beery. Mary C. Cline, widow of Elder John A. Cline, also a member of the group, claimed the period to be four weeks, which apparently included the entire time since the arrest at Moorefield. Sanger and Hays, *op. cit.*, p. 142.

40 Funk, *op. cit.*, p. 448. Also Nair, *op. cit.*, Chap. X, p. 24.

41. *Richmond Whig*, April 15, 1862.

42. Funk, *op. cit.*, p. 448. See also Acts 24:25.

43. *Ibid.* p. 452.

44. Henry Niswander, "Elder Kline as I Saw Him," *Gospel Messenger*, Vol. 61 (June 8, 1912), p. 358.

45. See Brunk, *Life of P. S. Hartman*, pp. 57 f. Also Sanger and Hays, *op. cit.*, pp. 156-58.

"Prisoners we are closely confined
But this not one of us should mind,
For Christ hath told us, in His Word,
That we should ever obey our Lord.

Chorus:

"We'll sure go home as soon as freed,
A holy life with God to lead;
Go home, go home, and that indeed
As soon as God the way will speed.

"We know it is God's holy will,
Our fellow men we should not kill
But we should lead a Christlike life,
And not spend all our days in strife.

"The Lord hath said we all can see,
Persecution we should flee,
And this we surely had in view,
A safer place we did pursue.

"But we were captured on our way,
And here as prisoners now we stay,
Absent from home and from our friends,
With no one near who pity lends.

"Dear Brethren all, both far and near;
Be with us all engaged in prayer,
That we from prison may be free,
And serve our God where'er we be.

"Although the world may at us look,
As though we too much undertook,
To leave our dearest friends behind,
And seek a safer place to find.

"But this we did for conscience' sake,
We did not wish God's laws to break,
For those, who will the Savior grieve,
Damnation surely will receive.

"But there is One who reigns on high,
That always will to us be nigh,
And if we put our trust in Him,
He will from prison us redeem.

"Then let us all the Lord obey,
That from the truth we never stray,
So that we may all stand the test,
And when we die go home to rest."

46. Sanger and Hays, *op. cit*, p. 81.
47. *Ibid.*, pp. 64 f.
48. *Ibid.*, pp. 143-46. See also Funk, *op. cit.*, p. 452.
49. Zigler, *op. cit.*, pp. 109-11. The writer has not been able to locate any April issue of the *Register*.
50. The *Register* suspended operations for five weeks, the last issue dated April 18. The types and other movable equipment and supplies were moved to a secret place in an adjoining county until Stonewall Jackson again secured the Valley from Union control. *Rockingham Register*, May 30, 1862.
51. Brunk, *Life of P. S. Hartman*, p. 60.

Chapter 6

1. Coulter, *op. cit.*, p. 467.
2. *Register*, Aug. 29, 1862.
3. *Ibid.*, Dec. 11, 1863.
4. Heatwole, *op. cit.*, p. 7.
5. *Daily Richmond Examiner*, June 26, 1862.
6. *Richmond Whig*, April 15, 1862.
7. Claims Commission, Claim No. 21843—Samuel Coffman.
8. Nair, *op. cit.*, Chap. X, p. 15.
9. Funk, *op. cit.*, p. 456.
10. Nair, *op. cit.*, Chap. X, p. 18.
11. Wright dealt mostly with the Quakers in this excellent work.
12. L. J. Heatwole in a letter to Wright claimed that Mennonites in Virginia used every opportunity to present appeals to the Confederate government or its representatives at home for recognition for the conscientious scruples against war. Heatwole letter to Edward Needles Wright, Nov. 5, 1928.
13. Zigler, *op. cit.*, pp. 95, 96.
14. *Ibid.*, p. 98.
15. Funk, *op. cit.*, p. 439.
16. Executive Papers, Box 438, July 22, 1861, Virginia State Library.
17. Funk, *op. cit.*, p. 446.
18. Zigler, *op. cit.*, pp. 99-101
19. Funk, *op. cit.*, p. 447.
20. Zigler, *op. cit.*, p. 101. See also Brunk, *Life of P. S. Hartman*, p. 58, and Sanger and Hays, *op. cit.*, p. 111.
21. Sanger and Hays, *op. cit.*, pp. 54-57.
22. *Journal of the House of Delegates of the State of Virginia for the Session*

of 1861-62, pp. 308-20. The votes of members are listed.

23. *Journal of the Senate of Virginia*, pp. 265-91.

24. *Acts of the General Assembly of the State of Virginia*, 1861-62, pp. 50, 51.

25. Brunk, *Life of P. S. Hartman*, p. 59.

26. Claims Commission, Claim No. 21844—Jacob Geil.

27. Sanger and Hays, *op. cit.*, p. 72.

28. Heatwole, *op. cit.*, p. 7.

29. Sanger and Hays, *op. cit.*, p. 111.

30. Wright incorrectly identifies B. F. Byerly as a Mennonite. See Wright, *op. cit.*, p. 203.

31. Zigler, *op. cit.*, p. 105.

32. Sanger and Hays, *op. cit.*, p. 82.

33. Zigler, *op. cit.*, p. 107.

34. *Ibid.*, p. 108.

35. Nair, *op. cit.*, Chap. X, p. 23.

36. Zigler, *op. cit.*, p. 109.

37. Funk, *op. cit.*, p. 179.

38. Zigler, *op. cit.*, p. 105.

39. Christian Good received his discharge on April 5, 1862 Original copy of Christian Good Discharge in possession of Paul S. Good.

40. Heatwole, *op. cit.*, p. 7.

41. Obituaries, *Herald of Truth*, Vol. 27 (Dec. 15, 1890), p. 380.

42. See page 31.

43. *Herald of Truth, op. cit.*

44. Breneman, *op. cit.*, p. 39. This source claims that Breneman had three horses shot from under him, each time making his escape.

45. Ethel Estella (Cooprider) Erb, *Through Trial to Crown of Life Story of Grandmother Heatwole Brunk Cooprider*. (Hesston, Kans.: Book and Bible Room, nd), p. 18.

46. See pages 56-60.

47. R. J. Heatwole, "Reminiscences of War Days," *Gospel Herald*, Vol. IV (Oct. 12, 1911), pp. 444 f.

48. R. J. Heatwole, "Civil War Story," Mennonite Historial Bulletin, Vol. IX (June 16, 1907).

49. See Heatwole, *op. cit.*, p. 8; Hartzler and Kauffman, *op. cit.*, pp. 214-15; Brunk, *Life of P. S. Hartman*, pp. 53 f. L. J. Heatwole actually does not name the individual he describes but the account is generally understood to refer to "Potter John." According to this account John D. Heatwole was repeatedly sought for by the military officials but in each case successfully eluded them. Eventually he "went far back into the mountains . . . alone where . . . his hiding place was located . . . and a squad of soldiers sent out to capture him. This squad of soldiers . . . was seen by a relative who reached Heatwole's place of concealment just in time for him to save himself by flight, but as snow was on the ground he was easily followed by his pursuers. After going some distance up a mountain ravine he then performed the feat of climbing to the top of a high mountain walking backwards in the snow and by this means threw his would-be captors off the trail the first night of his flight. . . . Not feeling safe to come back . . . he traveled over the numerous mountain ranges . . . until he

reached the eastern slopes of the Alleghany front. Here he came upon a people who treated him with great kindness and where he concluded to make his home. In due time these people learned something of the doctrine of the Mennonites and by means of a copy of the Confession of Faith which he had with him they became especially interested in the peace doctrine taught by the church. It only remains to state that at the close of the war the way was made open by the very means that drove this brother as a fugitive from military service to planting a church in this part of the state and it is here that appears the first meeting house built by Mennonites in West Virginia." Heatwole, *op. cit.*, p. 8.

50. War Department, Letters Received, No. 280-H-1863. Record Group 109.

51. *Confederate Statutes at Large*, II, p. 78.

52. *Daily Richmond Whig*, June 30, 1862.

53. Brunk, *Life of P. S. Hartman*, pp. 62, 63.

54. Nair, *op. cit.*, p. 35.

55. *Statutes at Large of the Provisional Government of the Confederate States of America*, Chap. 74, pp. 51, 52.

56. Zigler, *op. cit.* pp. 114, 115.

57. Sanger and Hays, *op. cit.*, p. 57.

58. Zigler, *op. cit.*, pp. 115-17.

59. *Ibid.*, 117-20.

60. *Ibid.*, p. 120.

61. Wright, *op. cit.*, p. 103.

62. *Journal of the House of Representatives. Journal of the Congress of the Confederate States of America*, Vol. V., p. 379.

63. Wright, *op. cit.*, p. 144. See *Journal of the State, op. cit.*, p. 228.

64. *Journal, op. cit.*, p. 431.

65. *Ibid.*, pp. 459-60.

66. *Ibid.*, pp. 489-90.

67. *Public Laws of the Confederate States of America. Confederate Statutes at Large. 1862-1864.* Chap. XLV, pp. 77-79.

68. See footnote 6.

69. Heatwole, *op. cit.*, p. 7.

70. Sanger and Hays, *op. cit.*, p. 83.

71. Cassel, *op. cit.*, p. 7.

72. Sanger and Hays, *op. cit.*, p. 164. Nair states that the "petitions to Congress and the personal friends of the petitioners who were well known in Congress must have created a confidence in that body that it was dealing with a people of such religious faith and integrity to principle that they could in no wise damage the Confederate cause." Nair, *op. cit.*, Chap. X, p. 45.

73. Wright, *op. cit.*, p. 105.

74. Wright describes in detail the activities of the Quakers in this respect, *Ibid.*, Chap. III.

75. Sanger and Hays, *op. cit.*, p. 73.

76. Zigler, *op. cit.*, pp. 121-22.

77. Wright, *op. cit.*, pp. 105 f. The *Rockingham Register* ran an advertisement placed by Captain P. H. Woodward for Mennonites and Dunkers in successive issues and also included a column calling attention to the advertisement and list-

ing requirements to qualify and procedures to pursue for exemption. See *Register*, Nov. 26, 1862.

78. Zigler, *op. cit.*, pp. 122-23. Peter Breneman, a well-to-do Mennonite in the Edom community, "spent most of his wealth by paying fines to keep his sons out of the service." Breneman, *op. cit.*, p. 11.

79. J. B. Jones, *A Rebel War Clerk's Diary*, Vol. I, p. 233.

80. Zigler, *op. cit.*, p. 123.

81. There is no record of Coffman's response to Hildebrand but Brunk concludes from Hildebrand's reply to Coffman that the latter was not in favor of such a day. Brunk, *History in Virginia, op. cit.*, pp. 165-66.

82. Wright, *op. cit.*, pp. 107, 108.

83. *Ibid.*, p. 110.

Chapter 7

1. Adjutant and Inspector General's Office. *Record of Exemptions in Virginia, 1862-63.* Chapter 1, Vol. 251.

2. Wright, *op. cit.*, p. 109.

3. *Richmond Daily Examiner*, Jan. 23, 1863.

4. Wright, *op. cit.*, p. 109.

5. Zigler, *op. cit.*, pp. 134-36.

6. James D. Richardson, *A Compilation of the Messages and Papers of the Confederacy*, Vol. I, p. 370.

7. *Richmond Daily Examiner*, Jan. 31, 1863.

8. Coulter, *op. cit.*, p. 319.

9. Zigler, *op. cit.*, pp. 138-41.

10. *Confererate Statutes at Large, 1862-1864*, p. 261.

11. *Official Records*, Series 4, Vol. III, P. 515.

12. Wright, *op. cit.*, p. 139.

13. Brunk, *History of Mennonites in Virginia*, Vol. I. p. 166.

14. D. H. Landis, Letter to Daniel Breneman written Oct. 30, 1864. *Herald of Truth*, Vol. I, December, 1864, pp. 81 f.

15. *Confederate Statutes at Large, 1862-1864*, p. 261.

16. Sanger and Hays, *op. cit.*, pp. 76 f.

17. John Brunk sent one son north through the mountains. Apparently this was Christian Brunk who was seventeen years of age in November, 1863. Claims Commission, Claim No. 21856—John Brunk. See also A. J. Fretz, *A Brief History of Bishop Henry Funck and Other Funk Pioneers* (Elkhart, Ind.: Mennonite Publishing Co., 1899), p. 187.

18. See pp. 72-73.

19. Claims Commission, Claim No. 16949—Estate of John Rhodes. Peter Heatwole went along "with his father's four horses and wagon of his own free will, because the soldiers were taking them to haul feed for the horses. When they were too poor to draw anything but empty wagons instead of allowing the soldiers to shoot them then he brought them home again and after long and careful feeding they were all right again." R. J. Heatwole, "Reminiscences of War Days. *Gospel Herald*, Vol. IV (Oct. 12, 1911), pp. 444 f.

20. Brunk, *Life of P. S. Hartman*, p. 61.

21. Claims Commission, Claim No. 9123—David Breneman.

22. Claims Commission, Claim No. 16500—Peter Blosser.

23. Heatwole, *op. cit.*, p. 7.

24. Claims Commission, Claim No. 21856—John Brunk.

25. Claims Commission, Claim No. 9521—Daniel P. Good.

26. *Register*, July 31, 1863.

27. Funk, *op. cit.*, p. 467.

28. *Register*, Oct. 9, 1863. Some of these details are secured from Beery's testimony made before the Claims Commission. Claims Commission, Claim No. 8941—Joseph Beery.

29. Claims Commission, Claim No. 8701—John Geil.

30. Zigler, *op. cit.*, p. 143.

31. Funk, *op. cit.*, p. 479.

32. It is claimed that Weavers Church was converted into a commissary for storing army supplies while the church grounds were occupied as a camping ground at times. L. J. Heatwole, "A Congregation of Mennonites That Has Existed for One Hundred Years," *Mennonite Yearbook and Directory*, 1927, pp. 29 f. See also H. D. Weaver, "Weavers Mennonite Church near Harrisonburg, Virginia," *Christian Monitor*, October, 1932, pp. 302, 303.

33. Heatwole, *op. cit.*, p. 7.

34. *Register*, Feb. 26, 1864.

35. *Ibid.*, March 4, 1864.

36. *Ibid.*, March 11, 1864.

37. *Ibid.*, March 18, 1864. This article relates actual incidents of consideration by Mennonites and/or Dunkers as follows: "Some time ago when flour was selling from twenty to twenty-five dollars at the mills I happened to notice a poor man hand over to one of the Tunker friends two ten dollar notes for a barrel of flour, and he returned him one of the tens. The same evening I saw a poor woman hand this same man money for a barrel of flour and I inquired afterwards how much she paid and I found she only paid ten dollars. I came directly to the conclusion that this man certainly is a loyal man to his country, although I never heard him open his mouth about his loyalty. . . . I am satisfied that this was not an exception to the general rule, but only one case out of many that I could mention where molasses, apple butter, corn, dry fruit and a variety of other necessaries of life have been sold to the poor and the refugees for less than half or one-third less than others."

38. *Ibid.*, Aug. 12, 1864.

Chapter 8

1. George E. Pond, *The Shenandoah Valley in 1864* (New York: Jack Brussel, Publisher, n.l), p. 24.

2. Claims Commission, Claim No. 16500—Peter Blosser.

3. *Official Records*, Series I, Vol, XXXVII, Part II, pp. 300 f.

4. *Ibid.*, pp. 328-29.

5. *Ibid.*, Vol XXXVIII, Part I, pp. 697-98.

6. *Official Records*, Series I, Vol. XLVIII, Part II, pp. 209-10.

7. P. H. Sheridan, *Personal Memoirs of P. H. Sheridan* (New York: Charles

L. Webster and Co., 1888), Vol. II. pp. 50-52.

8. Claims Commission, Claim No. 9527—Margaret Rhodes. Mrs. Rhodes claimed that in the confusion she evidently lost her vouchers for property taken by Union soldiers.

9. Sheridan, *op. cit.*, p. 52.

10. John W. Wayland, *Twenty-five Chapters on the Shenandoah Valley* (Strasburg, Va.: The Shenandoah Press, 1957), pp. 187-96.

11. John W. Wayland, *Virginia Valley Records* (Strasburg, Va.: Shenandoah Publishing House, Inc., 1930), p. 194. Wayland has a very detailed account of the Lt. Meigs incident in this volume, pp. 187-96.

12. Jonathan K. Hartzler, "A Visit to the Shenandoah Valley," *Herald of Truth*, Vol. 4, July, 1867, p. 106.

13. Wayland, *Virginia Valley Records*, p. 189.

14. L. J. Heatwole, *Scrapbook*, Part I, p. 48, EMC Mennonite Historical Library and Archives.

15. Michael Shenk, Letter of Nov. 19, 1864, *Herald of Truth*, December, 1864, Vol. I, pp. 82, 83.

16. Landis Letter to Daniel Breneman, *op. cit.*, pp. 81, 82.

17. Wayland, *Virginia Valley Records*, p. 194.

18. *Official Records, op. cit.*, pp. 307, 308.

19. Heatwole, *op. cit.*, p. 7. Emanuel Suter, one of the refugees in the group who went to Pennsylvania, wrote: "In looking over your valuable paper it afforded me much comfort and satisfaction to see where all my brethren and sisters are, who have left the Valley that I decided to subscribe for it. . . ." Letter to *Herald of Truth*, Vol. 2, January, 1865, p. 4.

20. Heatwole, *Scrapbook*, Part II, p. 48.

21. Landis Letter, *op. cit.*

22. Shank Letter, *op. cit.*

23. D. H. Landis loaded his family, their clothing and bedding, on a government wagon pulled by six mules, leaving their furniture and other possessions. Landis Letter, *op. cit.*

24. Among those who went along were seventeen-year-old Peter Hartman, the scarcely sixteen-year-old John S. Coffman, Samuel Showalter, and eighteen-year-old Christian Brunk. See Brunk, *Life of P. S. Hartman*, pp. 65-68; Claims Commission, Claim No. 21856—John Brunk, and Barbara Coffman, *op. cit.*, p. 51.

25. Heatwole, *Scrapbook*, Part II, p. 48.

26. Brunk, *Life of P. S. Hartman*, p. 67.

27. Pond, *op. cit.*, p. 199.

28. Landis Letter, *op. cit.*

29. Wayland, *Twenty-five Chapters*, pp. 230-31.

30. Brunk, *Life of P. S. Hartman*, p. 67.

31. Landis Letter, *op. cit.*

32. Brunk, *Life of P. S. Hartman*, p. 68.

33. Pond, *op. cit.*, p. 200.

34. Heatwole, *op. cit.*, p. 8.

35. *Register*, Nov. 11, 1864.

36. Wayland, *Twenty-five Chapters*, p. 388.

37. Earl R. Delp, Jr., "The Southern Claims Commission and the Claims of

Rockingham County Mennonites," Unpublished paper, EMC Historical Library and Archives.

Chapter 9

1. Arthur A. Elkirch, Jr., *The Civilian and the Military* (New York: Oxford University Press, 1956), pp. 102-4.

2. Wright, *op. cit.*, pp. 63-65.

3. Testimony of Daniel Heatwole in Claims Commission, Claim No. 9739—Samuel Shank.

4. Wayland, *Twenty-five Chapters*, p. 401.

5. Report of the Joint Committee on Reconstruction at the First Session, Thirty-Ninth Congress, Part II, p. 71. National Archives, Obviously Lewis includes Mennonites with Dunkers.

6. Richard Taylor, a Confederate Lieutenant-General, stated of these descendants of German settlers: "The devotion of all to the Southern cause was wonderful." Richard Taylor, *Destruction or Reconstruction*, ed. Richard Harwell (New York: Longman's, Green and Co., 1955), p. 47, as quoted by Earl Delp, Jr., *op. cit.* Confederate Commissioner Sidney Baxter described the group captured at Petersburg in March, 1862, among whom were many Dunkers and Mennonites as "all of Southern birth and all seem attached to the Southern cause." See pp. 53-54.

7. Fannie Rhodes, widow of John Rhodes, told of her son who was sent north before he was seventeen and who returned after the war and was threatened and chased by the "secesh" (secessionists), they "said we were lower than niggers." At a Dunker meeting a party of "secesh" abused him and others in the group who had been in the North during the war "calling them galvanized Yankees . . . beating them until others interfered." Not until Union authorities ordered such treatment to stop was the fear for young Rhodes relieved. Claims Commission, Claim No. 16949—Estate of John Rhodes.

8. *Digest of Disallowed Claims, 1876 Report*, Claim No. 21831, p. 248.

BIBLIOGRAPHY

A. PRIMARY SOURCES

1. *Official Manuscripts*

Unfortunately many Confederate Government manuscript records have been lost or destroyed. Some were captured and are desposited in the National Archives. Others are scattered throughout the United States. The following have been helpful in this study:

Adjutant Inspector General's Office (Confederate). Letters Received National Archives.

————. (Confederate). Record of Exemptions in Virginia. National Archives.

Civil War Claims Commission. Separate individual files on persons presenting claims for property loss due to Union military activies. National Archives. Very helpful in securing detailed experiences during the war.

Compiled Service Records of Confederate Soldiers Who Served in Virginia. National Archives.

Confederate Secretary of War. Letters Received. National Archives.

Special Order to Lieutenant Colonel J. R. Jones of the 33rd Volunteer Regiment of Virginia Militia from Major General Jackson. Historical Library and Archives. Eastern Mennonite College.

War Department (Confederate). Letters Received. National Archives.

2. *Official Publications*

Acts of the General Assembly of the State of Virginia.

Confederate Statutes at Large. 2 vols., 1864.

Digest of Disallowed Claims: Summary Reports of the Commissioners of Claims in all Cases Reported to Congress as Disallowed under the Act of March 3, 1871. 1873 and 1874 Reports. Old House of Representatives office Building, House File Room.

*Journal of the Congress of the Confederate States of America,
1861-1865.* Washington, 1905.

    Vols. I-IV—Journal of the Senate

    Vols. V-VII—Journal of the House

*Journal of the House of Delegates of the State of Virginia,
1861-1864.* Richmond.

Journal of the Senate of Virginia, Richmond, 1861.

*Report of the Joint Committee on Reconstruction at the First
Session, Thirty-Ninth Congress.* National Archives.

Richardson, James D. *A Compilation of the Messages and Papers
of the Confederacy* (1861-1865). 2 vols.

*Statutes at Large of the Provisional Government of the Confederate
States of America,* Richmond, 1864.

War of the Rebellion: Official Records of the Union and Confederate Armies. 128 serial volumes. National Archives. Although
dealing with military activities, this voluminous work gives much
information on many other activities in the Confederacy.

3. *Mennonite Church Sources*

Minutes of Virginia Mennonite Conference Including Some Historical Data. Scottdale, Pa.: Mennonite Publishing House, 1939.
Very scanty information available here.

*The Confession of Faith of the Christians Known by the Name
of Mennonites with Nine Reflections by Peter Burkholder.*
Translated from the German by Joseph Funk. Winchester, Va.,
1837. Historical Library and Archives, Eastern Mennonite College.

4. *Diaries, Journals, and Memoirs*

Funk, Benjamin (ed.). *Life of John Kline, Collated from His
Diary.* Elgin, Ill.: Brethren Publishing House, 1900.

Jones, J. B. *A Rebel War Clerk's Diary.* 2 vols. Philadelphia:
J. B. Lippincott & Company, 1866.

Sheridan, P. H. *Personal Memoirs of P. H. Sheridan.* 2 vols.
New York: Charles L. Webster, 1881.

5. *Letters and Narratives*

Blosser, Abraham. "A Historical Sketch of the Early Mennonites in Virginia," pp. 129-42 in *History of the Mennonites* by Daniel K. Cassel. Philadelphia: Daniel K. Cassel, 1888.

Bright, Captain P. R. Letter to Governor Letcher. Written on June 6, 1861. Executive Papers, Virginia State Library.

Brunk, Christian and Emanuel Suter. "A Letter from Virginia." Aug. 14, 1865, *Herald of Truth*, Vol. II, October, 1865.

Brunk, Harry A. *Life of Peter S. Hartman Including His Lecture on Reminiscences of the Civil War and Articles by the Hartman Family.* Published by the Hartman Family, 1937.

Hartzler, Jonathan K. "A Visit to the Shenandoah Valley." *Herald of Truth*, Vol. 4, I, July, 1867, p. 106. ─────────

Heatwole, L. J. Letter to Edward Needles Wright. Nov. 5, 1928. Historical Library and Archives, Eastern Mennonite College.

─────────. "The Virginia Conference." Chapter XIII in *Mennonite Church History* by J. S. Hartzler and Daniel Kauffman. Scottdale, Pa.: Mennonite Book and Tract Society, 1905.

─────────. Scrapbook. Historical Library and Archives, Eastern Mennonite College.

─────────. "A Congregation of Mennonites That Has Existed for One Hundred Years." *Mennonite Yearbook and Directory*, 1927, pp. 29 f.

Heatwole, R. J. "Reminiscences of War Days." *Gospel Herald*, Vol. IV (Oct. 12, 1911), pp. 444 f.

Hildebrand, Jacob. Letter from Hermitage, Augusta County, Virginia. Oct. 24, 1864. *Herald of Truth*, Vol. II, January, 1865, p. 3.

─────────. Letter to J. M. Breneman. Written May 15, 1865. *Herald of Truth*, Vol. II, ───────── , 1865.

Kline, John. Letter to Governor Letcher. Written July 22, 1861. Executive Papers, Virginia State Library.

Landis, D. H. Letter to D. H. Breneman. Oct. 30, 1864. *Herald of Truth*, Vol. I, December, 1864, pp. 81 f.

McCue, I. M. Letter to Governor Letcher. Written July 20, 1861. Executive Papers, Virginia State Library.

Maupin, Colonel William A. Letter to Governor Letcher. Written July 19, 1861. Executive Papers, Virginia State Library.

Niswander, Henry. "Elder Kline as I Saw Him." *Gospel Messenger*, Vol. 61 (June 8, 1912), p. 358.

Shenk, Michael. Letter of Nov. 19, 1864. *Herald of Truth,* Vol. I, December, 1864, pp. 82 f.

Suter, Emanuel. "A Letter from Lancaster Co., Pa." Dec. 30, 1864. *Herald of Truth,* Vol. II, January, 1865.

6. Newspapers

Daily Richmond Whig, 1862.
Richmond Daily Examiner, 1861-62.
Richmond Dispatch, 1861-64.
Richmond Whig, 1861-64.
Rockingham Register, 1860-65. This publication is an indispensable source for accounts of local events and for community sentiment.

B. SECONDARY MATERIALS

1. General Civil War History

The historian concerned with any phase of Civil War study must begin with the general histories of the period. The most exhaustive of these are:

Channing, Edward. *History of the United States,* Vol. VI. New York: The Macmillan Company, 1925.

McMaster, John Bach. *History of the People of the United States during Lincoln's Administration.* New York: D. Appleton-Century Company, 1927.

Nevins, Allan. *The Ordeal of the Union.* 2 vols. New York: Charles Scribner's Sons, 1947.

————. *The Emergence of Lincoln.* 2 vols. New York: Charles Scribner's Sons, 1950.

————. *The War for Union.* 2 vols. New York: Charles Scribner's Sons, 1959-60.

Randall, James G., and David Donald. *The Civil War and Reconstruction.* Boston: D. C. Heath and Company, 1961.

Rhodes, James Ford. *History of the United States from the Compromise of 1850,* Vol. III. New York: The Macmillan Company, 1895.

The most useful of these general treatments are Nevins' excellent volumes which are interestingly written and are the product of more recent thorough research. The earlier intensive work by Rhodes is still useful but is becoming increasingly outdated. Randall's one-volume work completed by Donald is also thorough in its treatment of the war period. These general histories are basic to any meaningful study of the period but they provide virtually nothing on the history of the religious objectors to war.

2. Histories of the Confederacy

Scholars concerned with developments within the Confederacy will find the following volumes an indispensable part of their study:

Coulter, E. Merton. *The Confederate States of America, 1861-1865.* Vol. VII of *A History of the South* by Wendell Holmes Stephenson and E. Merton Coulter (eds.). 10 vols. Baton Rouge: Louisiana State University.

Eaton, Clement. *A History of the Southern Confederacy.* New York: Macmilliam 1954.

Roland, Charles P. *The Confederacy: The Chicago History of American Civilization.* Daniel Boorstin (ed.). Chicago: The University of Chicago Press, 1960.

3. Religious Objectors in the Civil War

The above histories of the Confederacy make scarcely any reference to the religious objector and his role in the war. Much less do they give any attention to the Mennonites as a separate group. Coulter and Eaton make only passing reference to religious objectors in connection with the April 16, 1862, Confederate conscription law. Roland makes no reference to them whatsoever. The most intensive study on the subject is that of Edward Needles Wright, *Conscientious Objectors in the Civil War*, Philadelphia: University of Pennsylvania Press, 1931. Wright gives more attention to the Quakers but his information on the Mennonites, as well as on other groups who conscientiously opposed war, is very useful. His work is scholarly and reliable. However, it should be revised to incorporate the materials made available since 1931.

A thorough study of Mennonites in the Civil War has never

been made, either as they related to the Union or to the Confederacy. This thesis is an attempt to provide such a study of Mennonites in the Confederacy. In addition to Wright, the following have been very helpful in securing information concerning the religious objector groups:

Brunk, Harry A. *History of the Mennonites in Virginia*, Vol. I. Harrisonburg, Va.: published by the author, 1959.

Sanger, S. F., and D. Hays. *The Olive Branch of Peace and Goodwill to Men.* Elgin, Ill.: Brethren Publishing House, 1907.

Sappington, Roger E. *Courageous Prophet.* Elgin, Ill.: The Brethren Press, 1964.

Wayland, John W. *A History of Rockingham County.* Dayton, Va.: Ruebush-Elkins Company, 1912.

————. *Twenty-five Chapters on the Shenandoah Valley.* Strasburg, Va.: The Shenandoah Press, 1957.

————. *Virginia Valley Records.* Strasburg, Va.: Shenandoah Publishing House, Inc., 1930.

Zigler, D. H. *History of the Brethren in Virginia.* Elgin, Ill.: Brethren Publishing House, 1914.

4. *Other Published Secondary Materials*

Bender, Harold, "Peter Burkholder," *The Mennonite Encyclopedia*, I, pp. 477 f. Scottdale, Pa.: Mennonite Publishing House, 1956.

Breneman, Charles D. *A History of the Descendants of Abraham Breneman.* Elida, Ohio: published by the author, 1939.

Brunk, Harry A. "Samuel Coffman," *The Mennonite Encyclopedia,* I, p. 634. Scottdale, Pa.: Mennonite Publishing House, 1955.

Cartland, Fernando. *Southern Heroes of the Friends in Wartime.* Cambridge: The Riverside Press, 1895.

Coffman, Barbara. *His Name Was John: The Life Story of an Early Mennonite Leader.* Scottdale, Pa.: Herald Press, 1964.

Davis, Julia. *The Shenandoah.* New York: Farrar and Rinehart, Inc., 1945.

Dowdey, Clifford. *The Land They Fought For: The Story of the South as the Confederacy, 1832-1865.* Garden City, New York: Doubleday and Company, 1955.

Ekirch, Arthur A., Jr. *The Civilian and the Military*. New York: Oxford University Press, 1956.

Erb, Ethel Estella (Cooprider). *Through Trial to Crown of Life: Story of Grandmother Heatwole Brunk Cooprider*. Hesston, Kans.: Book and Bible Room, nd.

Fretz, A. J. *A Brief History of Bishop Henry Funck and Other Funk Pioneers*. Elkhart, Ind.: Mennonite Publishing Company, 1899.

Hardesty's Historical and Geographical Encyclopedia. Description and Lists of Virginia Military Regiments. Richmond: H. H. Hardesty and Company, Publishers, 1884.

Heatwole, Manassas (Obituary). *Herald of Truth*, Vol. 27 (Dec. 15, 1920), p. 380.

Lonn, Ella. *Desertion During the Civil War*. New York: The Century Company, 1908.

Mumford, Beverly B. *Virginia's Attitude Toward Slavery and Secession*. Richmond: L. H. Jenkins, 1909.

Nicolay, John G., and John Hay. *Abraham Lincoln—A History*. 10 vols. New York: The Century Company, 1890.

Pond, George. *The Shenandoah Valley in 1864*. New York: Jack Brussel, Publisher, nd.

Stackpole, Edward J. *Sheridan in the Shenandoah: Jubal Early's Nemesis*. Harrisonburg: The Stackpole Company, 1961.

Waddell, Joseph A. *Annals of Augusta County, Virginia:* From 1726 to 1871. Staunton, Va.: C. Russell Caldwell, Publisher, 1902.

Weaver, H. D. "Weavers Mennonite Church, near Harrisonburg, Virginia." *Christian Monitor*, Vol. XXIV (October, 1932), pp. 302 f.

Wenger, Joseph H. *History of the Descendants of J. Conrad Geil and His Son Jacob Geil*. Elgin, Ill., nn, 1914.

Wiley, Irvin Bell. *The Common Soldier in the Civil War. Book II, The Life of Johnny Reb*. New York: Grosset and Dunlap, 1943.

Wooster, Ralph A. *The Secession Conventions of the South*. Princeton: Princeton University Press, 1962.

Yearns, Wilfred Buck, *The Confederate Congress*. Athens, Ga.: The University of Georgia Press, 1960.

5. *Unpublished Materials*

Coffman, Nellie. "A Short Biography of Samuel Coffman." Historical Library and Archives, Eastern Mennonite College. (nd)

David, Ronald. "The Virginia Mennonites and the Civil War." Historical Library and Archives, Eastern Mennonite College. May 21, 1957.

Delp, Earl R. "The Southern Claims Commission and the Claims of Rockingham County Mennonites." Historical Library and Archives, Eastern Mennonites College. May 12, 1962.

Morgan, Edith Wenger, "Stories My Father Told Us." Unpublished pamphlet in possession of Mrs. Earl Grove.

,Nair, Charles E. "John Kline." Unpublished manuscript in possession of Agnes Kline, Bridgewater, Va. 1952.

Shenk, Virginia Ann. "A Statistical Study of Claims Made to the Southern Claims Commission by Residents of Augusta and Rockingham County." May 28, 1962. Mennonite Historical Library and Archives, Eastern Mennonite College.

INDEX

A

Adjutant Inspector General's Office, 83, 85
Agrarian way of life, 18, 111
Albemarle County, 64
Anderson, B. F., Confederate Congressman, 78
Aristocracy of eastern Virginia, 20
Arrest, 51, 56, 58, 72, 73, 74, 91, 122n39
  Attempts at, 46
Ashby, Turner, Confederate Cavalry Commander, 76
Ashe, Thomas S., Confederate Congressman from North Carolina, 79
Atlanta, Georgia, Battle of (1864), 100
Augusta County, 15, 16, 23, 48, 81

B

Baldwin, John B., Confederate Congressman, 77, 79, 81
Banks, Nathaniel, Union General, 60, 75
Baptism, 16
Baxter, Sydney, S., Confederate War Department, 53, 54
Baylor, George, Member of Virginia House of Delegates, 69
Beery, Henry, 27, 91
Beery, John, 43, 44
Beery, Joseph, 27, 39, 44, 57, 58, 91
Bell, John, Constitutional Union candidate in 1860, 23
Benjamin, Judah, Confederate Secretary of War, 68
Blosser, Abraham, 39, 81, 101, 120n2
Blosser, Peter, 26, 39, 51, 89, 96, 121n11
Blue Ridge, 76, 107, 108
Blue Ridge Rebellion, 63-64
Bond, Captain, 51
Botetourt, County, 69, 78, 83
Breckinridge, John, 23
Breneman, David C., 26, 40, 89
Breneman, Melchiah, 29, 73, 125n44
Breneman, Peter, 127n78
Brethren (See Dunkers)
Bright, P. R., Confederate Captain, 28, 29
Brock's Gap, 90
Brunk, Christian, 127n17, 129n24
Brunk, George, 39, 44
Brunk, Harry A., 8, 10, 88

Brunk, G. Henry. 43. 73-74. 89
Brunk, John, 27, 40, 42, 45, 89, 127n17
Brunk, Samuel, 30, 38, 118n8
Bureau of Conscription, Confederate, 83
Burkholder, Martin, 48
Burkholder, Peter, 16
Burkholder, Simon, 44
Byerly, Benjamin, 71, 87

C
Campbell, John A., Assistant Secretary of War, 19, 88
Capture, 10
Castle Lightning (See Confederate Prisons)
Castle Thunder (See Confederate Prisons)
Chambersburg, 98
Chancellorsville, Battle of (1863), 96
Church leaders, 10, 72, 93, 112
Church records, 8
Civil liberties, 7, 19, 111
Civil War Claims Commission, 8, 26, 42, 114-115
Cline, J. M., 122n38 and n39
Cline, Mary C., 122n39
Cline, Samuel, 81
Coakley, Daniel J., 39
Coakleytown, 102
Coffman, Samuel, Mennonite bishop, 26, 37, 44, 48, 64, 66 photograph, 83, 112,
    117n3
Coffman, William A., 62
Compiled Service Records of Confederate Soldiers, 29-31
Confederate Congress, 77-82, 84, 85, 86, 87, 88, 93
Confederate Constitution, 25, 26
Confederate military forces, 50, 51, 56, 76-77, 96-110
Confederate prisons
    Castle Lightning, 53
    Castle Thunder, 53, 55 (photograph), 91, 121-22n27, 122n35
    Libby Prison, 52-53
Confession of Faith (so-called Burkholder Confession), 17, 81
Conscription Act, Confederate (1862), 38, 75-84; (1864), 87, 88
Cooperation: with Dunkers, 16; with government, 10, 28-39, 40
Commissary wagons, 89
Contribution of supplies to Confederate soldiers, 90
Coulter, E. Merton, 53, 55
Confederate Senate, 79-80
Cross Keys, Battle of, 76-77
Charlottesville, 97
Custer, George A., Brigadier, 101
Coffman, John S., 129n24

D

Dale Enterprise, 102
Dayton, 101, 102
Davis, President Jefferson, 19, 86
Department of Northern Virginia (Confederate), 47
Depots, 41-46
Deserter gangs, 22, 47-61, 89, 121n9
Desertion, 21, 22, 29, 32, 41-46, 47-61, 62, 73, 74, 112
Details, 32; aiding others to desert, 43, 63, 91; with help of Union soldiers, 45; detailed as teamsters, 38; to work at shoemaking, 38; to work on Baltimore and Ohio Railroad, 38; to help furnish nitre to Confederate government.
Disloyalty to Confederacy, 63-64, 78
District of the Shenandoah, (Confederate Military district), 47
Destruction in Valley (1864), 96-110
Dortch, William, Confederate Senator, 78
Douglas, Stephen A., Senator from Illinois, an anti-secessionist Democratic candidate in 1860, 23
Driver, David, 27
Dunkers, 9, 16, 40, 77, 79, 80, 104, 107, 122
  beliefs, 16, 23, 26, 28, 34, 35, 37, 81
  churches, 48, 77-79, 83
  deserters, 47-61, 63
  sentiment toward, 36, 37, 63, 75, 94-95, 114
  leaders, 23, 65, 67-69, 77-78, 86-87, 115

E

Early, Jubal, Confederate Lieutenant General, 97-108
Edom, 39
Ekirch, Arthur, A., Jr., 10
Escape (See Flight)
Ewell, Richard S., Confederate General, 76
Exemption from military service, 8, 28, 39, 50, 65-84, 85, 87, 88, 89, 93, 109, 113, 126-27n77
  Confederate Exemption Law, 80, 88, 92
  Ineligible for, 54, 73
  January, 1863, Exemption Bill, 85-87
  Public manifestation of gratitude for exemption, 83-84
  Virginia Exemption Law, 69-70, 75, 82

F

Families, 21, 109; Mennonite, 16, 29, 38, 42, 43, 71; of soldiers, 54, 101, 102
Farmers, 20, 89, 90
Fishers Hill, 100
Flight, 10, 41-46, 48, 50, 73-74, 89, 92, 103-109, 112
Foragers, 96-97
Fort Sumter, 24
Foster, Thomas J., Confederate Congressman from Alabama, 79
Frank, David, 31, 74, 118n15

141

Franklin, Western Virginia (later West Virginia), 51, 76, 78, 122n35
Franzl-Sigel, Union Major General, 96
Fremont, John C., Union General, 76
French, Colonel S. Bassett, Aide-de Camp to Governor Letcher, 34, 35, 36
Front Royal, 76
Fugitives, 51, 57
Funk, Benjamin, 82
Funk, John S., 121n9
Funk, Jonathan, 121n9

G

Geil, Henry, 40
Geil, Jacob, Mennonite deacon, 39, 40, 42, 46, 70-71
Geil, John, Mennonite bishop, 26, 30, 46, 48, 83, 117n9
German inhabitants of Shenandoah Valley, 20, 24, 93, 130n6
Gettysburg, Battle of (1863), 29, 73, 86
Good, Christian, 30, 32, 125n39
Good, Daniel J., 26, 43, 44, 45, 118n11, 120n2
Good, Daniel P., 27, 43, 44, 89
Gordonsville, 97
Government, 10, 17, 18
Gray Algernon, Member of Virginia House of Delegates, 69, 81, 82
Graybill, Jonas, 77
Greene County, 64
Guides, 41-46
Gratton, Charles, Member of Virginia House of Delegates, 69
Grant, Ulysses S., Union General, 96, 97, 98, 99, 107
Guerrilla forces, 99-100, 108

H

Hardy, County, Virginia (later West Virginia), 48
Harlan, James, Senator from Iowa, 18
Harpers Ferry, 76
Harris, John T., 67, 87
Hartman, David, 43
Hartman, P. S., 32, 33, 51, 60, 70, 89, 106, 107, 108, 109, 129n24
Heatwole, Abraham. 27
Heatwole, Gabriel, Sr., Mennonite minister, 30, 51, 57, 58
Heatwole, Gabriel D., 27, 44, 114-115, 118n11, 120n2
Heatwole, Henry, 119n42
Heatwole, Jacob, 119n42
Heatwole, John D., 30, 74, 125-26n49
Heatwole, L. J., 16, 32, 38, 71, 74, 81, 92, 101, 104, 106
Heatwole, Manassas, 31, 54, 73
Heatwole, Peter, 31, 127n19
Heatwole, R. J., 89
Heatwole, Shem S., 30, 119n42
Heatwole, Simeon, 27, 51, 52, 71, 121-22n27

Herald of Truth, 103, 129n19
Hiding, 10, 29, 41-46, 72-73, 92, 120n2; return from hiding, 83
Hildebrand, Jacob, Mennonite bishop, 48, 83, 88
Hopkins, John, Member of Virginia House of Delegates, 53
House of Delegates (Virginia General Assembly), 69
Hunter, David, Union Major General, 96, 97, 98, 99

I

Illinois, 74
Imboden, John D., Confederate Brigadier General, 97
Imprisonment, 10, 15, 52-60, 74; release of prisoners, 83

J

Jackson, T. J. (Stonewall), Confederate General, 20, 21, 34, 35, 43, 47, 68, 72, 75, 96; death, 96, 124n50; Jackson's military forces, 53, 58, 60, 72
Johnson, Edward, Confederate General, 76
Johnston, Joseph E. Confederate General, 47
Joint Committee on Reconstruction, 113-114
Jones, J. R., Lieutenant Colonel, 35

K

Kernstown, 58, 60, 98
Keyser, Western Virginia (later West Virginia), 48, 49 (map), (See also folded map.)
Kline, John, Dunker elder, 23, 25, 37, 57, 58-60, 64-68, 77, 82, 83, 122n39; murder of, 91-92

L

Lancaster County, 73
Landis, D. H., 103, 129n23
Lawlessness in local area, 92
Lee, Robert E., Confederate General, 20, 21, 96, 97, 99
Letcher, John, Governor of Virginia, 23, 24, 28, 35, 38, 65-66, 68, 86
Letter delivery, 45
Lewis, Charles, 68
Lewis, John F., 113
Libby Prison (See Confederate Prisons)
Lincoln, Abraham, President of U.S., 18, 24, 25, 68
Local sentiment, 39, 60, 63, 64, 91, 94-95, 104
Lonn, Ella, 22
Losses from Sheridan's raid, 110
Lynchburg, 97

M

Mail route, 39
Manassas, First Battle of, 47 (See folded map)
Manassas Gap Railroad, 32 (See folded map)

Martinsburg, Virginia (later West Virginia), 104, 108, 109
Maryland, 76, 97
May, Henry, 91
McCauseland, John, Confederate, Brigadier General, 98
McClellan, George B., Union General, 47, 96
McDowell, 76
Meigs, John R., Lieutenant, 101, 104, 129n11
Mennonite deserters, 29-31, 34-41, 47-61
Mennonite churches in Maryland and Pennsylvania, 64; in Shenandoah Valley,
   48, 63, 92
Mennonite Conference (1864), 103
Mennonite preaching in western Virginia counties (later West Virginia), 48
Merritt, Wesley, Union Major General, 100
Mexican War, 15
Militarism of South, 111
Military service, 15, 18, 28, 29, 36, 37, 38, 74, 112; return from military service,
   83; local men in military service in 1861, 11n32
Military strategy, 19-20
Miller, David, 52, 121n11
Miller, David M., 71, 121n18
Miller, Joseph A., 52, 54, 56, 71
Mitchel, Leonard, 44
Monterey, 52, 89, 122n35
Moomaw, B. F., Dunker elder, 37, 69, 77, 83, 87
Moorefield, Pendleton County, Virginia (later West Virginia), 56, 122n39
Mosby's Rangers, 22, 99-100
Mount Crawford, 27, 49 (map), 107 (See also folded map)
Mount Jackson, 32, 37, 49 (map), 56, 122n38 (See folded map)
Murder of John Kline (See John Kline)
Muster fines, 28

N
Nair, Charles E., 71
National Archives, 9
Nazarenes, 80
Newtown, 108
New Market, 72; Battle of (1864), 96, 108
Nieswander (Niswander), Joseph E., 38
Nieswander, Jacob, 53-54
Niswander, Henry, 59
Noncooperation with government, 41
Nonresistance, 17, 18, 29, 36, 81
North, 18, 19, 64, 73, 91, 100, 112, 113
North Mill Creek, 51
North Mountain, 107, 108

O
Oakland, Maryland, 48, 49 (map)

Officials, 8; Confederate 16, 45, 53, 63, 64, 83, 89, 99, 112; state (Virginia), 16, 65, 67, local, 58, 81, 82, 89, 110, military, 67, 74, 91, 112, 117n3
Ohio, 48, 73, 103 (See folded map)

P

Page County, 39, 64
Passes secured to go North, 106, 107 (photograph)
Pendleton County, 34, 48, 50, 56
Peninsular Campaign, 47, 96
Petersburg, Hardy County, Virginia (later West Virginia), 44, 48, 49 (map), 50, 51, 82, 89, 121n18, 122n35 (See folded map)
Petersburg, South of Richmond, 99
Petitions: Dunkers and Mennonites to Virginia General Assembly, 69; Dunkers and Mennonites to Confederate Congress, 77-78; Dunkers of Botetourt, Roanoke, and Franklin Counties to Confederate Congress, 78; Quakers of North Carolina to Confederate Congress, 78; other petitions (memorials), 78-79, 85, 124n12
Piedmont, 100
Pilots, 41-46, 89
Postmaster, 39; "Postmaster" of "Underground Railroad," 45
Port Republic, 76, 107
Potomac River, South Branch, 51
President, 85
Preston, William, Confederate Congressman from Virginia, 85
Prisoners' Song, 59, 123-24n45
Providing for the needy, 94

Q

Quakers, 8, 16, 18, 19, 33, 35, 40, 65, 75, 78, 79, 82, 84
Quartermaster General's Office, 83

R

Railroads: Baltimore and Ohio, 38, 48, 98, 104; Central Railroad of Virginia, 52, 97 (See folded map).
Rebellion, 7, 16, 18, 38, 113
Recognition by government, 10, 62-84
Referendum on secession, 24, 25, 26, 27
Refugees, 41-46, 73, 94, 103-109
Requisitions, Confederate, 90; Union, 97, 98, 102
Revolutionary War, 15
Rhodes, David E., 27
Rhodes, Frederick, 27, 30
Rhodes, Henry A., 30
Rhodes, Henry H., 45
Rhodes, Henry L., 27, 38, 40, 42, 45, 50
Rhodes, John, 43, 46, 89

Rhodes, John J., 46
Rhodes, Margaret, H., 29, 43, 45, 101, 129n8
Rhodes, Rush, 54
Richmond, 19, 21, 51, 52, 54, 55, 56, 58, 59, 71, 72, 73, 81, 83, 87, 91, 96, 98, 122n35 (See folded map)
Richmond Civil War Centennial Committee, 53
Richmond Whig, 26, 75
Riley, John, 44
Rockfish Gap, 100
Rockingham County Courthouse, 35, 57 (photograph), 58
Rockingham Register, 24, 36, 37, 60, 90, 92, 124n50
Rutherford, John C., Member of Virginia House of Delegates, 69
Russell, Charles, Confederate Congressman from Virginia, 87

S

Sanger, S. F., 71
Scotch-Irish inhabitants of valley, 20
Secession, 9, 16, 18, 23-27, 69, 91, 113
Secessionists, 46
Sectional rivalry, 18
Secretary of War, Confederate, 68, 83, 85, 88, 93
Selling of provisions to poor, 90, 128n37
Senate (Virginia General Assembly), 69
Shank, Jacob, 50
Shank, Jacob, Jr., 27, 40
Shank, Michael, 30, 33, 102
Shank, Samuel, Mennonite minister, 26, 40, 44, 113
Shenandoah County, 48
Shenandoah Mountain, 51
Shenandoah Valley: as a strategic area, 20, 32, 41, 47, 48, 49 (map), 96, 99 (See also folded map)
Sheridan, General Philip H., 10, 21, 99-110
Sherman, William T., Union General, 106
Shields, James, Union General, 76
Showalter, J., 53
Showalter, Jackson, 122n38
Sickness, 64-65
Slavery, 16, 26
Smith, William, Confederate Congressman from North Carolina, 79-80
Sparrow, Edward, Senator, Confederate Senator from Louisiana, 79
Stanly, George W., 39
Stanton, Edwin, Secretary of War, 18
Staples, Waller, Confederate Congressman, from Virginia, 86
Staunton, 51, 52, 89, 97, 100, 102, 122n35
States Rights, 18, 113
Strasburg, 76
Substitutes, 34, 38-40, 75, 86, 87, 91, 112; fees for, 119n46
Suter, Emanuel, 27, 71, 129n19

Suter, Jacob, 31
Swift Run Gap, 60

T

Taxes, 26, 69-70, 78, 79, 80, 84, 87, 89, 93
Teams pressed into service, 52, 89, 127n19
Teamsters, 34, 36, 38, 69-70, 71, 80, 113
Threats by secessionists, 26-27, 64, 92, 130n7
Thurber, William, 82
Thurman, W. C., 81
Tom's Brook, 108
Torbert, Alfred T., Union Major General, 100, 107
Train (large group of deserters), 45
Tunkers (See Dunkers)

U

Underground Railroad, 41-46, 50
Union, 7, 17, 18, 20, 21, 23-24, 25, 36, 38, 41, 98
Unionist, 8, 46, 91, 92, 110
Union military forces, 20, 21, 32, 47, 48, 60-61, 63, 72, 76-77, 96-110, 113-115
Union sentiment, 18, 24, 25, 104
Union lines, crossing of, 43, 44, 72, 92

V

Valley Campaign (1862), 47-48, 60, 76-77; (1864) 96-110
Vicksburg, Battle of, 86
Virginia General Assembly, 68, 77, 78, 80, 86
Virginia Secession Convention, 23, 24, 25, 27
Vouchers, 99

W

Wagon train, 106-109, 129n23
War of 1812, 15
Washington, D.C., 19, 20, 21, 76, 97 (See folded map)
Wayland, John W., 101, 110, 113
Waynesboro, 72, 100
Weaver, David, 31, 119n42
Weaver's Church, 29, 42, 103, 128n32
Wenger, Benjamin, 101
Wenger, Henry, 31
Wenger, Henry M., 31, 33, 54 (Wanger)
Wenger, Isaac, 40
Wenger, Jacob, 26, 30, 43, 54 (Wanger)
Wenger, Levi, 44, 50, 89
Wenger, M. H., 50, 89
Wenger, Noah, 27, 101
Wenger, Peter, 44
West Virginia, 15, 25, 41, 48, 97

147

Winchester, 20, 32, 33, 37, 47, 49 (map), 76, 108
Wine, Jacob, 91
Woodson, John C., Member of Virginia House of Delegates, 68
Woodstock, Shenandoah County, 56, 107, 108
Worship in secrecy, 92
Wright, Edward Needles, 8, 65, 82
Writ of habeas corpus, 111

Z
Zigler, D. H., 50

DATE DUE

DE 13'78			
GAYLORD			PRINTED IN U.S.A.